HANDO'S GWENT

EDITED
BY

CHRIS BARBER

A CENTENARY TRIBUTE TO FRED HANDO

— THE ARTIST/HISTORIAN OF GWENT.

To John.
With best Wishes
Chris Barber

First Published 1987

ISBN Hardback 0 9510444 4 3
ISBN Softback 0 9510444 5 1

Cover designed by Derek Lawton

BLORENGE
·BOOKS·

3, Holywell Road, Abergavenny, Gwent
NP7 5LP. Tel: Abergavenny 3909.

Printed by South Western Printers Ltd.
Caerphilly, Mid-Glamorgan, South Wales

To the memory of Fred Hando
the artist/historian who was
a true 'Man of Gwent'
and his son Robert who accompanied
him on many of his journeys.

Llandogo — The Sloop Inn

CONTENTS

"This Gwent of ours owes much of her charm to her shyness. Around even her hilltop hamlets she erects a screen of trees, her gracious and ancient homesteads are rarely visible from the main roads, and the loveliest of buildings — those little grey churches — are withdrawn into the most secret haunts.

Haunts where bird-song and brook-music accompany the hymns, where the flowers of the hedgerows are culled for the decoration of font and screen, window-ledge and altar table, and where the good folk are called to worship by the same bells which called their fore-fathers to church when the first Elizabeth was queen."

Fred J. Hando.

FOREWORD

The first day I ever went to school I was run over by a bull nose Morris motor car. I wasn't run all over, just my little foot but it was a close call. I was just four years old and having experienced four years of this wicked world you were expected to look after yourself and walk the couple of miles to school and back and keep your face and hands clean at all times. To get yourself run over by a bull nose Morris was your stupid fault and qualifed you for a clip around the ear hole. Well that was just about the measure of life in the elementary schools of 1920. They were hard and ruthless institutions. I hated school. There were sixty children to a class with one teacher. Life at school was a running battle between that poor teacher and the sixty ragamuffins that he beat into submission, or tried to, every minute of every day. There were some very nice teachers and there were some dreadful ones and you were stuck with just one teacher for a whole year. That same depressed face, that awful shiny suit was presented to you at nine o'clock every morning and you were stuck with it for a year until you moved up from standard one to standard two. One teacher to sixty little devils.

Johnny Morris making a speech, keenly watched by his old headmaster — Fred Hando.

Of course you couldn't be treated as an individual; you were a potential source of trouble and had to be smacked down. I served a seven year sentence in that school and at the most mature age of eleven moved on to the new school on the hill — Hatherleigh. By then I was a pretty experienced old lag. I knew every trick in the book. Just let them try that's all just let them try. That was my attitude. I was well conditioned for rebellion. But, I had not met Fred Hando and the teachers he had gathered around him. To start with you were called by your christian name. That was unheard of in the old prison. The old prison was built to contain little rascals, the windows were high in the walls to stop you looking at the world outside. But Hatherleigh was an old mansion with wonderful views over the Bristol channel. It was relaxed and not tense. Boys and girls were mixed together. We had different masters and mistresses for different lessons. We were considered as people. Life had entirely changed, I actually looked forward to going to school and being with all those lovely human beings who understood and were kind. Fred Hando unlocked our prison doors and set free what talents that I am sure would have remained locked in us for ever. Fred was a most talented man. He proved to us that all things were possible. Of course you can sing, of course you can play the piano, of course you can write an essay, of course you can draw a drawing and paint a picture. Go on do it. Well, you see Fred could do all these things and he and his staff did their best to show us that there was more to this life than arithmetic and history. We all of us come to cross roads in our lives. I can only hope that at every cross roads there will be a smiling Fred Hando pointing the way and saying "This is the most pleasant and interesting way" He did it for me. Thank you, Fred.

Johnny Morris

INTRODUCTION

It is with great pleasure that I have compiled this centenary tribute to the work of Fred Hando, for whilst typing the manuscript I found my mind drifting through a myriad of childhood memories recalling family outings in a slow, black Morris 8, following traffic-free roads to numerous destinations in deepest Gwent. Our esteemed leader was Fred Hando who had generally made a prior arrangement with the owner of a historic manor house for us to pay a call and examine the house and grounds.

One such occasion that comes to mind was the day that we visited Trewyn, the home of Mrs. Molyneux where we gazed at oil paintings of ancestors spanning four centuries; including famous soldiers and administrators and one sixteenth-century lady who lived for 162 years! We poked our noses into the remarkable octagonal pigeon-house, containing 832 nesting holes which were reached by an ingenious revolving ladder and we pondered with sadness on the graveyard of the family pets. I was entranced when I stood and watched Fred sketching details of the house with deft strokes of his pencil to provide a rough outline which would form the basis of the final drawing which he would complete at home. We then adjourned for afternoon tea, handling with care Mrs. Molyneux's delicate bone china before driving back to Newport in the gathering gloom of a late November afternoon.

Chris Barber (at the age of eight) sketching in the company of Fred Hando on one of his journeys in Gwent.

I was only eight at the time, but I was already an admirer of Fred Hando and how I wished that I could draw like him. In later years when I began exploring the Gwent countryside on my bicycle I read his books avidly and took delight in following in his footsteps and on a few occasions I was even able to suggest locations to him that were worthy of a visit.

It was in 1983 that a vague thought came to me that I would like to compile a book about Fred Hando and acting on an impulse I wrote to Robert Hando who was Fred's son from his second marriage. I had of course known Robert as a youngster on our joint family outings and also as fellow pupils at Newport High School.

We spoke on the phone one evening and I outlined my ideas for a book and asked Robert if he had any of his father's drawings in his possession. He promised to have a rummage in his attic and then come back to me. However the months passed by and I heard nothing so I assumed that Robert had either forgotten or lost interest in the matter so I turned my attention to another project.

It was a year later that I received a letter from a Newport solicitor informing me that Robert had recently died (in his early forties) and had left a note suggesting that I was contacted for I had an interest in his father's sketches and writings.

Subsequently I arranged to buy the copyright of the Hando material from Robert's widow Susan and work on the book began in earnest with a view to publishing it in time for 1988 — the centenary of Fred Hando's birth.

When Fred Hando first began exploring and writing about Gwent it was an era of sleepy hamlets with oil lamps flickering in cottage windows and the pubs were mainly frequented by local farmers and country characters, all with fascinating stories to relate. Fred was able to capture the spirit of those times, recording for posterity the legends, local stories and historical associations. He visited and sketched hundreds of historic houses and cottages — many of which have since been renovated and "improved" so that the original flagstone floors, oak beams and inglenook fireplaces can no longer be seen.

Following in the footsteps of Archdeacon William Coxe whose classic volume "Coxe's Tours in Monmouthshire" was published in 1801, Fred conspired with the noted historian Sir Joseph Bradney and met frequently with the mystical writer Arthur Machen.

It was a lifetime's work, and Fred devoted all his spare time to tramping around his home county, recording his findings and sketching everything that caught his eye. He wrote with a distinctive style — 'old fashioned' perhaps by today's standards but poetic, entertaining and vividly descriptive. Sometimes he was criticised by other historians for taking local assumptions or legends and writing them as history, but he was rarely dry and his enthusiasm for his subject was infectious.

Hardly a stone was left unturned for there were very few locations in the county that Fred failed to visit and record. Towards the end of his life he made frequent sorties over the border, for by that time he was finding it hard to feature locations that he had not already covered in Gwent. His final article for the South Wales Argus was delivered just a fortnight before his death in February 1970.

It is interesting to consider now, how day-to-day life and attitudes have changed since Fred first began to describe the history and scenery of Gwent. Since those days there has been a tremendous increase in traffic and the Severn Bridge brings more and more visitors to Gwent. Many of the old rural bus services and the country railways have disappeared yet today there is a far greater interest in walking and exploring the countryside. Guided walks, waymarked trails, picnic sites, country parks and viewpoints have been provided and the importance of the conservation of wildlife and habitats is widely recognised.

Fred Hando was a man ahead of his time — an artist historian with a personal mission to explore and record a land that he loved passionately. He gave his readers of that era considerable pleasure which I now wish to revive and provide an opportunity for a new generation to appreciate and enjoy the remarkable record compiled by this man of Gwent.

Chris Barber
October 1987.

THE CONTENTS

Faced with a pile of nearly 800 articles and other material written by Fred Hando over several decades it was an enormous and at first bewildering task for me to decide how to piece this book together. Eventually I decided to compile it in the form of a series of journeys dealing with selected areas of the county but covering the whole of Gwent, which the reader can easily follow.

Many readers will of course ask — "Why wasn't so and so church, castle, house etc included?" or, "Why haven't I featured the occasion when Fred visited their house back in 1952? Obviously I have had to be selective and already I have thoughts on the possibility of compiling a second volume which will include such items as Pontypool Grotto, the Buck Stone, the Kymin Naval Temple and various historic houses etc. etc. So hopefully in due course volume two will be available.

Chris Barber.

CHAPTER ONE

Fred Hando — 'Man of Gwent'

The three sons of Alfred and Miriam Hando in about 1913.
Fred (aged 25), Frank (18) and Harry (23).

Fred Hando was the eldest of three sons born to Alfred and Miriam Hando on the 23rd of March 1888. The middle son, Harry became a successful stock broker and formed the partnership of Robgent and Hando in Newport. Frank the youngest son became a local government officer. Their father Alfred Hando was Deputy Postmaster of Newport Post Office and Miriam was his second wife.

As a young boy Fred attended school in Maindee, a suburb of Newport and in later years he joined the staff there and specialised very appropriately in English and Art. As a young man he was a fairly notable sportsman who displayed particular skill in rowing, wrestling and long distance running.

The Hando family came from North Curry in Somerset and during the nineteenth century one part of the family emigrated to Australia. Sadly the parents died on the long journey and their two five-year-old sons stepped ashore alone in the world. Fortunately some kind soul took care of them and today hundreds of their descendants can be found in Australia.

In the First World War Fred served in the Royal Engineers and was at Arras and Vimy Ridge acting as a Gunnery Officer.

Fred married Alice Stanton the daughter of a Newport builder and they had two children called Margaret and John, but sadly Alice died whilst still quite young.

In 1925 Fred was appointed as the first headmaster of Hatherleigh Road school in Newport and his style of teaching was unusual for those times being of a "progressive" nature. Whilst maintaining a strong discipline in the school, Fred was still able to enjoy a close and friendly relationship with his staff and pupils. Hatherleigh was a school where boys were taught to cook and girls learned how to do woodwork.

Hatherleigh School

Pupils from Hatherleigh School still remember the time when a new gymnasium was opened by the Mayor of Newport and to everyone's delight, headmaster Fred celebrated the occasion by going hand over hand up the climbing ropes.

Miriam Andrews who once taught at Hatherleigh remembers Fred as "a very witty man who said things with his tongue in his cheek. He was a wonderful headmaster and he made the children proud of Hatherleigh."

Fred was also interested in church affairs and was organist and choir-master at Summerhill Baptist Church, Newport for many years. He was indeed a man of many talents for he was a teacher, a writer, an artist, a musician and a historian with a very special love and affinity for the countryside and antiquities of Gwent.

After a number of years as a widower, Fred married Daisy who was one of his staff at Hatherleigh and very soon a son was born who they named Robert.

In his long association with the South Wales Argus he wrote the amazing total of 795 articles about the county that he loved so much. He devoted a lifetime to recording its history, treasures and characters, bringing pleasure to many thousands of readers. His last article was published on February 13th 1970, a few days before his death. He had produced the series with very few breaks for seventeen years.

Many of the articles were republished in the seven books which were published by the Newport firm R.H. Johns over the years. However a considerable amount of his writings and sketches did not appear in book form and so for the first time since their appearance in the South Wales Argus extracts from these articles are contained in this new book, timed to commemorate the centenary of the birth of Fred Hando.

Fred Hando died on Tuesday 17th February, 1970 at St. Joseph's nursing home in Newport. He was 81 years of age.

Shortly after his death a fund was set up by the Monmouthshire Local History Council and the South Wales Argus to establish several memorials to perpetuate the memory of Fred Hando. The money collected was used to establish a number of Hando seats at vantage points in the county that were considered by Fred himself to be particularly fine.

Daisy (Ysiad), young Robert and Fred Hando outside the gates of Buckingham Palace on the day in 1953 that he received the M.B.E. for his services to education and to Monmouthshire.

A few words from Fred..... "How it all began."

In 1922 I submitted my first article, with a sketch to Mr. W.J.T. Collins editor of the Argus. He accepted it and suggested a series, to be known as *Rambles in Gwent*. Since that series ended I have sent in articles as the spirit moved me.

I consult the accepted authorities which are placed at my disposal by Mr. John Collett, Newport Borough librarian and his excellent staff. Primed with this knowledge I spend as much time as possible on the spot, sketching the buildings, etc. and especially, getting to know the people.

In general, the people of Gwent are enthusiastic and helpful, as witness the charming young ladies of Chepstow who were anxious to push me into an underground passage which, they were sure, led to Henry Martin's tower in the castle.

You will find at least one "card" in every village. His activities vary. Sometimes you will hear of a special society — say a "society of leisure." Sometimes you will notice an advertisement appearing in the window of the inn on the entry of a brewery director. Or again, you will listen to some mysterious legend which the "card" hopes that you will publish. Not long ago, however accompanied by friends, whom I will call Bob and Tommy, I met the genuine prefabricated "card."

We three were admiring the Elizabethan doorway of the Robin Hood Inn at Monmouth. Suddenly a short, slight man joined us. " Excuse me gentlemen," he said, "you seem greatly interested in this ancient inn. You know, I suppose, that it is 30,000 years old?"

He was a complete stranger to us, but bowing to his local knowledge, I invited him to tell us more.

He continued: "This street, gentlemen, is Monnow Street. It is packed with history. Up there, in the shadow of old St. Mary's, is where Nelson fought Napoleon D. Bonaparte. I was present at the battle, which you will remember, gentlemen, Nelson won hands down. After the battle they shook hands, then came down to the Robin Hood for dinner. They invited me to join them."

"The following morning," he went on, "I saw Nelson leave by coach, and I said to my friends, we shall not see his like again. But gentlemen, I talk too much. I suppose you gentlemen are architects — or surveyors?"

"No", I answered casually, "this" — pointing to Bob — "is Mr. Sherlock Holmes. This — Tommy — is Dr. Watson, and I am Dr. Watson's secretary."

Not at all perturbed, the card begged the honour of shaking hands with us for he had read all about us in the "Strand" magazine. Later he regaled us and pulled out a thick wad of notes, remarking how fortunate he was to have married Solly Joel's daughter.

On another occasion I was attacked by a gentleman enveloped in whisky fumes, who accused me of being a blood-stained snooper from Whitehall. Then there was the time when an irate farmer armed with a knobbly stick gave me precise and picturesque views about trespassers, but he became interested in my questions about prehistoric camps and tracks in his fields.

After a long talk he asked: "Why do you waste your time down here in the valley? Get up on the hillside there and follow the Roman road. I'll bet you a crown that road is at least a hundred years old!"

I once had an embarassing moment in 1922 when the rumour spread that the Mormons were persuading Monmouthshire girls to cross the Atlantic with them. Now while I was sketching the old inn at Ponthir the inn-keeper's wife came out "to pass the time of day."

As we talked I noticed that a curtain in the bar-parlour was drawn aside and one of the maids was gesticulating frantically. After a time this maid came out, caught her mother by the hand and drew her away, saying: "Mother, you can't be too careful with these mormons about."

Sugar loaf and Abergavenny from the slopes of Blorenge

The Ancient Kingdom of Gwent

Gwent is the southern gateway into Wales. Until 1535 it was a part of Wales, as it is clear that Nature intended it to be. In that year Henry VIII abolished the authority of the Lords Marcher, and the twenty-four Lordships between the Usk and the Rhymney were taken to form the new county of Monmouth. Legally therefore in England, Monmouthshire is in Wales as far as sport, education and religion are concerned. In some parts of the county "Eden's tongue" is heard still, and the lovely old place-names reward careful study.

Washed on the south by the Severn Sea, Gwent is bordered on its sides by mountains and rivers; on the east by the Wye, on the north-east by the Monnow, by the Black Mountains of Brecknockshire on the north, and on the west by the River Rhymney. From the flats of Caldicot and Wentllwg, the land rises by gentle hills in the centre to the ranges and peaks of the Black Mountains. Many of the hills are surmounted by the circular or oval camps of our early races; many of the ranges are traversed by ancient ridgeways. The ridge from Newport almost to Chepstow was clothed with the great forest of Wentwood, for many years a royal Chase. Our valleys, formed by streams flowing from the heights, are full of charm. Some in the north-west have been changed into smoke-laden channels of industry, but even there much beauty remains. Others, like the Cwm near Shirenewton, resound to birdsong and watermusic.

Gwent

Black
Mountains
Llanthony
Cwmyoy
Grosmont
Skirrid Fawr
Sugar Loaf
Skenfrith
Monmouth
Abergavenny
White Castle
Ebbw Vale
Blaina
Blorenge
Blaenafon
Llanover
Tredegar
Trellech
Llandogo
Raglan
Tintern
WYE VALLEY
Usk
Pontllanfraith
Pontypool
Llantrisant
Devauden
Newbridge
-on-Usk
Aberbeeg
Crumlin
St Arvans
Wentwood
Chepstow
Caerleon
Abercarn
Ponthir
Cwmfelinfach
Risca
Newport
Catsash
Sudbrook
Caldicot Level
Caldicot
Christchurch
Rogiet
Bassaleg
Llanwern
Nash
Redwick
St Mellons
Marshfield
St Brides
Peterstone
Wentllwg Level
Mouth of the Severn

CHAPTER TWO

Through the Vale of Usk

Caerleon — Bulmoor — Kemeys Inferior — Gypsy Tump — Llantrisant — Llanllowell — The Three Salmons, Usk — Llancayo Windmill — Trostrey — Bettws Newydd — Coed-y-Bwnydd — Llangattock-nigh-Usk. Returning via — Llanellen — Llanover — Mamhilad — Llanfihangel Pontymoile — Croesyceiliog — Llanfrechfa and Ponthir.

Our journey starts from the Ship inn near the bridge across the Usk on the B4595. Follow the road past the inn to reach Old Caerleon and turn left along the Bulmoor Road.

"At the turn of the road." Caerleon seen from St. Julian's.

On a sunny, breezy June afternoon we left Caerleon Village ("Ultra Pontem") and took the Bulmoor Road. How does Arthur Machen describe it? *"That most wonderful, enchanted delicious road that winds under the hillside, under deep Wentwood, above the solemn curves and esses of the river."* No over-statement this seemed to us as we looked to the left over the river and upwards to the Graig.

At **Bulmoor** we stopped. Here on the left, was a Roman graveyard. Here was found the stone with the inscription: *"Ave, Julia, Casissima conjux; inaeternam vale."* (Hail, Julia, dearest wife; farewell for ever.)

Here to my delight, were to be seen still, in the ancient barn the cider-mill and press which, as a boy, I had seen at work, with the patient horse pulling the circular stone around and around, until at last the farm lad could collect the "muss" in his sack and place it under the press, so that the last drops of golden liquor might be squeezed out. The mill was still in use two years ago.

On now we drove into ever lovelier glades, while the river reflected Glen Usk and Ivybridge, and the hills above. Grass in the meadows grew knee-high, foxgloves and campions higher and a sparkling "nant-y-mynydd" came tinkling down on the right. Then we came to **Kemeys.**

A rough lane led up to the right, and became rougher as we approached the walled orchard and garden. Mrs. Morgan greeted us and showed us first the famous inscription on the barn.

1597

E. XXXIX R.

The Stone portrait of George Kemeys

Then we inspected the stone portrait of George Kemeys, erected in 1623. I noted with dismay that since my last visit, the right hand of the figure had broken away. If, after three hundred and more years, the stone is about to weather, I suggest that the tablet should be removed indoors.

It is dated 1623 and shows the figure of a gentleman dressed in Tudor costume — the costume of thirty years before. In one hand he holds an hour-glass, in the other a parchment roll, and a scroll bears the words: ONVS WHVTH AWEL FE TERFYN AMSER (Unless the wind blows, time will cease). In the top right-hand corner of the tablet are the arms of the Kemeys family, and the initials G.K. of George Kemeys.

What the significance of the Welsh motto may be, we know not. But the expression on the face of that jolly old cavalier we shall not forget. Three hundred years old, his smile is still fresh and engaging today. As we watched him, we thanked Heaven that Cromwell's marauders had not visited Kemeys!

Kemeys House, had a right-of-way passing through to a church. At Kemeys this was alongside the stone channels which conveyed, and still convey, the waters of the stream which descends from Kemeys Graig, which waters are used in the dairy for cleansing the milk utensils.

It seems clear that the present house, old as it is, was not the first on the site, for a couple of stone stairways must have belonged to an earlier building. Crowned by its Elizabethan chimneys, Kemeys House extends north-east and south-west, quite 150 feet above the river. The porch rises to the full height of the main structure, but is marred by a hideous extension to the north-east. Many of the original windows survive, with their hood-mouldings above, but some have been filled in to evade the window tax.

On my first visit to Kemeys with Colonel (later Sir Joseph) Bradney, we entered through the doorway surmounted by the stone portrait. On the wall within, nine or ten feet above the floor, was a series of long wooden pegs.

I suggested to the Colonel, himself a giant, that there were even more gigantic giants in those days. "Those pegs my son," he rejoined, "were for stretching harp-strings."

Entering to-day by the dairy doorway, we admired the water-channels in the floor, and the great beams in the ceiling. This room, together with others now separated by partition walls, formed the hall.

Of the other rooms on the ground floor, the most interesting is the south room, containing the ceiling plastered in high relief. This I am glad to report, is in excellent preservation, and although small, remains one of the finest of our late seventeenth century ceilings.

We climbed the great stairs to the first landing and inspected the three panelled oak doors and the primitive plaster figures on the walls. These extraordinary figures are obscured by many coats of whitewash, but my host promised to "clean them up", and then I hope to find exhibits which will compete with the monstrosities of the best modern exhibitions.

Up on the attic floor we moved carefully from room to room, while the bats fluttered around us. Lath and plaster walls contrasted with the original walls, a yard and more in thickness. A beautiful Tudor portal opened on to steps leading nowhere; another set of steps lead downward to a vertical shaft.

This shaft is probably the origin of the legends associated with secret passages. Old inhabitants of Kemeys believed that there was such a passage to the church, continuing under the river to the Garn, also in the opposite direction under Wentwood to Penhow Castle.

Another pretty theory was that smugglers brought their goods by river to the secret passage, and hence to the foot of the shaft, up which the goods were hoisted to the attic. We know now that these shafts and passages were convenient ways of disposing of household refuse.

Like all our Monmouthshire hosts, Mr and Mrs Morgan had been kind and helpful to us, and were obviously taking care of their vast home. After thanking them, we jolted down the lane and halted at the churchyard gate. Meditation in perfect silence is difficult. Gentle background sounds lull the unquiet upper chambers of the mind and only then may one contemplate in peace.

All Saints' church, Kemeys Inferior.

So it was that in God's acre of Kemeys, with the sweet songs of the river and the birds rippling the surface of the great silence, we became again attired in our rightful stillness of soul. And that is the great gift of Gwent to the townsman — tranquillity, serenity, calm.

Across the Bulmoor road, almost lost amid great trees and precariously near the river, grey, old, mysterious, stands the little church of **Kemeys Inferior.**

This Kemeys is "Inferior" to Kemeys "Commander," beyond Usk. Payn de Kemeys served under Hamelyn in the Norman conquest of Gwent in 1901, and possibly built his home at Kemeys Commander. Later, the family settled at Kemeys Inferior, which, in Welsh, is Kemeys "Fach" or Kemeys "Isha."

Yet the name was known in this land long before the Conquest, for a king of Glamorgan in the Seventh Century had his court at Cemeis. It is assumed that Payn de Kemeys was a Welshman who fought on the side of the invaders.

We know that Edward was lord of Kemeys manor in the Thirteenth Century, that his descendants married into the Beauchamp, Cecil, Lewis and Jones (Herbert) families, that they counted among their numbers sheriffs and M.P.s for the county and that the last of them was George Kemeys, builder of the "Folly," who died in 1722.

"All Saints" was the family church. The family throughout the ages descended the stone steps from their massive porch and continued through their orchard down to the grey sanctuary overlooking the river.

There was a right-of-way from the summit of Kemeys Graig through the house to the church. A mountain brook marked this way through the house and joined the Usk near the church.

Yet there was no memorial to a Kemeys! George Kemeys sold his manor to Lawrence Lord in 1700 and the memorials which we remember were chiefly to members of the Lord family.

The church was a nave, chancel, north chapel, south porch and single bell-turret. Sadly it is no more, but the stones which formed it and which had given five centuries and more service on the green "ynys" of Kemeys are being transported to the summit of Stow Hill in Newport, where they will be used in the extension of the cathedral.

Now there were a pile of stones, the door, a couple of stone columns, the screen of trees and the river; and one bird in the tallest tree twittered a requiem.

Gypsy Tump.

We halted at **Gypsy tump** once again to savour its mystery. Was it a burial ground, or a sighting point, or a fortress? Only excavation could answer these questions, but what a happy hunting-ground it has been for picnicking children!

The river on its journey down from Newbridge sweeps across to salute the Tump and then executes a graceful bend towards Plas Llecha while the trees, deep-rooted in the red earth of the tumulus, envelope us in green shade.

Llantrisant church.

A little rise and there, tucked in cosily among the greenest hills dreamed **Llantrisant.** The name implies "church of the three saints", David, Padarn and Teilo, and the farmhouses sleep around the church like grey chicks around a grey hen. This delectable hamlet has been for me a favourite port of call. So green it is, so sweetly cradled in our lovely river valley, so snugly sheltered from the east winds by the Wentwood ridge! So delightful the approach, either along the Bulmoor road, or via Glen Usk and Tredunnock or from Usk! And always on arrival, such a welcome in the Royal Oak or the Greyhound.

One of the fireplaces at the Royal Oak.

In the spacious bar of the **Royal Oak** the carpenter's craft is displayed well in ceiling and fireplace, as shown in my sketch. The cross-beams and some of the lighter longitudinal beams bear plain "stops," as also does the chamfer on the splendid oak lintel above the fire-place, which beam is 8ft. 6in. long and 1ft. 2in. wide. The fireplace deserves close study. There is no trace left of the bake-oven which I feel must have existed to the left but the quoin-stone — I almost wrote "menhir" — on the left, cut and chamfered to perfection, serves its purpose admirably. On the other side two stones form the quoin and the remainder of sides and back is built with cut stones — all limestones.

The big oak lintel beam has survived the fires of centuries, acquiring with time a rich patina. In the fireplace is seen the handsome iron fire-container brought, so Mrs. Jeremiah informs me, from Bertholey house. A similar fireplace in the dining room has a iron fire-back inscribed "E.I. 1743."

Before leaving the bar my hostess showed me her grandfather clock, made by D. Evans of Pontypool, with an inset of a sailing ship rolling one roll per second; a brass falcon perch (see small sketch) found in her cider-house; a magnificent cross-bow with horn-sights; a mole trap, and the ship's bell of the Llangibby Castle, presented to her when the vessel was broken up.

We climbed the ancient circular stairs to the pleasant bedrooms with their views over the pastoral countryside. Thence another flight took us to the attic-floor where the great timbers stand giving no sign of strain after 2½ centuries (for the roof was raised about 1700 A.D.). It seems probable that a shaft ran from the attic down to the cellar, and that drainage from the cellar floor was washed into an underground stream which is known to flow under the house. Here, then, is another instance of the early form of sanitation introduced by the monks.

In the churchyard is the graceful modern cross, standing on the original chamfered base with five steps. Two semi-circular archways lead into the church, one at the foot of the tower, the other in the porch, and above the porch entrance is the sundial dated 1718.

In the tower without, and on the west wall of the nave within, are fixed stones with the inscription:

1593

E R XXXV

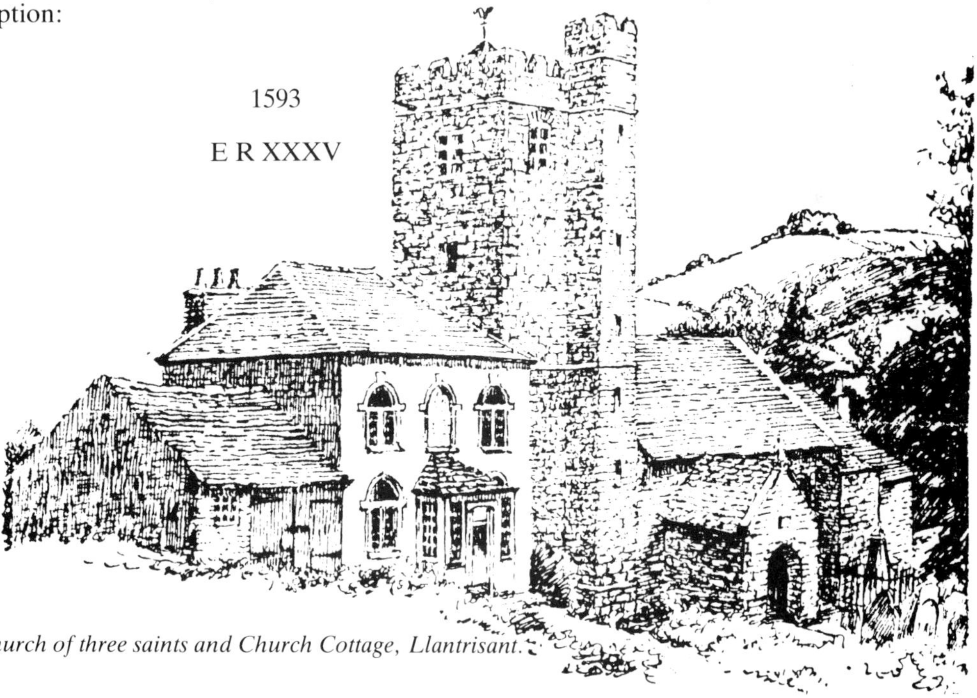

The church of three saints and Church Cottage, Llantrisant.

(the 35th year of Queen Elizabeth's reign). These, and the stone in the barn at Kemey's Inferior, show the pride felt by the people of this remote county in their great Queen, whose navy had five years before inflicted such a signal defeat on the Armada of Spain.

Adjoining the tower is a projecting turret, the slit windows of which light the spiral stairs leading up to the battlements. There are two bells, dated 1622 and 1829.

The inner doorway of the porch has a stone into which a beautiful consecration cross is cut. Within the church the sun shines on the tombstones forming part of the floor, and all is simple and plain. This was — still is — a church of the countryfolk, and the few wall monuments emphasise this fact. An inner sense perceives the spirit of this holy place, compounded of the hopes and fears and prayers of the thousands of Llantrisant folk who have worshipped here during six centuries.

Passers-by see only the north side of **Llanllowell church,** with its leaning chimney, and windows of two widely separated periods, but the view of the porch, the south wall and the bell-turret on that sunny morning was of pure delight, intensified by the heady scent of syringa which grows luxuriously in the churchyard.

St. Lewellyn's church, Llanllowell, near Usk.

I opened the gate under the depressed arch of the porch and was about to open the inner door, when I paused in astonishment. The lintel of this inner doorway, was obviously an early Christian monument. I examined it with care and was able to discover the incisions shown in my sketch. Comparing it with the stones illustrated and described by Dr. Nash-Williams in his *Early Christian Monuments of Wales* I noted that there was only one other stone with a similar six-pointed incised cross, and it seems that the Llanllowell stone was missed by Dr. Nash-Williams in his survey of the Monmouthsire monuments.

As shown in my drawing, two of the stones on the doorway bear consecration crosses, while in the north wall of the nave is a good example of a thirteenth-century window. An earlier window may be seen in the west wall. The font and the inner arch of the south entrance are also Norman, while the projection on the south wall houses the steps leading to the rood-loft which has disappeared. Of the two bells, both modern, one only is in use.

There was a church at Llanllowell in 1254, when Mr. Maurice was the rector. Usk Priory owned land in the parish in later years, and in 1603 it was recorded that "William Nicholas, Gent, holdeth it, allowing the curate 40s. per annum."

Incised lintel, consecration crosses and thirteenth century window at Llanllowell.

For many travellers memories of **Usk** centre around the **Three Salmons.** To Thoresby-Jones, Usk was the natural jumping-on centre for trips to Caerleon, Abergavenny, Monmouth and Chepstow. He found the old borough of considerable historic interest but what was more important to the wayfarer was that Usk contained "one of the most comfortable and intelligently contained hotels in all the border — the venerable Three Salmons."

The Three Salmons, Usk.

In season he tells us, he was offered fresh Usk trout for breakfast and a choice between Usk Salmon and Severn Salmon for dinner. The beds were soporific and *"if you do — after salmon — remain wakeful you will find a judicious selection of books in your bedroom."*

It seems that until salmon fishing became "the thing" the old inn was known as the Golden Cross. This may well have been for it stands where the Roman roads cross, one facade on Bridge Street, the other on Porthycarne Street. Like all big solid Silurians, its hands are warm, and some of my pleasant memories are of meals at the Salmons after driving many miles in mid-winter.

Indeed its reputation for cosy warmth was the reason why for many years the autumn sessions would adjourn to the inn after the court-house was too cold.

Today, with its entrance lounge, two bars, three dining rooms, a TV room, 12 bedrooms, a ballroom and a vast cellar in 3 compartments (used as an air-raid shelter during the last war), the Three Salmons makes a happy port of call for the traveller, the historian, the artist, and especially the angler.

Turn right by The Three Salmons Hotel in Usk to follow the A471 past the ruined windmill at Lancayo.

The windmill at Llancayo.

There is a splendid shell of a windmill at **Llancayo,** near the Usk-Abergavenny road (A471), in a great field which forms part of the 350 acre farmland of Mr. Evan Williams, of Llancayo Farm.

We examined the windmill within and without. The walls are 2ft. 2in. thick, the diameter at ground level is 28ft., and this diminishes through the 56ft. height in such a way as to produce an impression such as an observer receives on viewing a Doric column.

Skill of a high order lay behind the planning and construction of this graceful tower, with its cut-stone circles, each slightly wider than the circle above, each stone sloping slightly inwards, its brick-arched window heads, its two stone string courses, and its windows indicating the five floors of the tower.

At the summit of the tower, precariously perched, is a segment of a toothed wheel: another relic protudes below the upper string-course. Behind the mill, from pole to pole, extend the wires conveying electric power from Glascoed to Llancayo.

Said farmer Williams, "I often look at those wires and the windmill, and see them as a symbol of the revolution that has taken place in industry in so short a time." That is true, but by the beginning of this century the doom of the windmills and watermills could be foreseen, and soon the steam-driven mills, the steel rolls replacing the millstones, and the vast new mills in our ports had rendered the old mills uneconomic.

That is why we in Monmouthshire look with delight on our surviving watermills, some of whose owners assure me that they have sufficient orders to justify "a seven-day week and a 24-hour day."

Llancayo windmill was a tower or "smock" mill, in shape similar to a rustic's smock. At the summit the "cap" was arranged to support the shaft and the sweeps and to rotate so that the sweeps faced the wind. This type of mill appeared first in the sixteenth century, but as I have been unable to find a picture of its sweeps and other equipment I cannot date it.

Signs of a fire are evident throughout the interior. Of the varied stories given me, the most probable tells how on a still summer morning the miller went to market leaving his sweeps coupled to the gearing. A sudden fierce wind sent the sails rotating rapidly, the red hot coupling and brakes ignited the timber and the mill was a flaming torch before the miller returned.

About 1 mile beyond Llancayo turn up a narrow lane on the right to reach Trostrey church.

The Church and Cross — Trostrey

On that calm silvery afternoon a great peace brooded over **Trostrey** hill top. The trees west of the church, in pale-green leaf, held choirs of birds, whose music deepened the sense of peace; the springtime tents of hills and woods, seen through the silver April light, augmented the magic. "Here," I thought, "in this remote country church, our people came to worship in the days of Elizabeth and Cromwell, of Malborough and Nelson. Here during the dark hours of the Battle of Britain they prayed.

It is worth climbing Trostrey hill if only to see the churchyard cross. While the cross itself is modern (for our ancient crosses were destroyed in 1643) the steps are original, and remind us of the part played by crosses in village life. At the wayside crosses engagements were made, and bargains struck; from the churchyard crosses the news was proclaimed every Sunday morning; processions ended at the cross, loved ones were buried near it, and on the feast days it was festooned with flowers. In some instances the cross is older than the church, and always it holds a place of deep reverence in the hearts of the village folk. It is forbidden to remove or damage this, one of the most sacred of our ancient landmarks.

Inside the church I found a wall-tablet inscribed in memory of Captain Charles Hughes of Trostrey who fought "for his Majestie against ye rebelles" and died, aged 57, in 1676.

Contine from Trostrey church to reach the quiet village of Bettws Newydd.

"Betws" is a bede-house, an oratory, a resting place for worship and prayer. Near **Bettws Newydd** church was traditionally an old building used as a rest-house for travellers and pilgrims; this may have given the village its name. Old itself, it must have replaced one still older.

In the churchyard is something older, maybe, than bede-house or church. Opening the wicket-gate alongside the mounting-block, I saw ahead two yew trees, one sedate and well-balanced, the other, on the right, appearing to be chaliced in some extraordinary grey material. Closer inspection showed that the present yew tree has grown up from the ruins of another, immensely old.

Hów old? Knowledgeable countryfolk tell me that they allow 4ft. in girth for the first 150 years of growth, and 2ft. 6in. for each succeeding century.

I am often asked why yew trees are found in our churchyards. Without doubt their sombre colour rendered them appropriate, but there is a deeper reason. Dr. Vaughan Cornish brackets the yew with the last sheaf in the reaping-field as one of the earliest symbols of immortality, and we know that in the fifth century the space between the yew tree and the church was a sanctuary "as inviolable as the interior of the church."

There is no truth in the legend that the wood of the yew was used by archers. Our bowmen used elm for their bows, and of course churchyard yews were planted long before wood was used for bows.

This lovely old church at Bettws Newydd was founded in 1188 by Aeddan of Grosmont but there is no known dedication. The present church is shorter than the original building. Stone seats in the porch, an oaken door studded with "blacksmith's" nails, holes for a slip-bar within the doorway, iron bars protecting most of the windows, a Norman font with decorations consisting of concentric semi-circles and cable, a piscina and bracket in the chancel, and many other items give character to the church, quite apart from its main glory.

This is the superb pre-Reformation screen and rood-loft, which I have attempted to portray for you. By great good fortune, and by virtue of its remote location this marvellous specimen of mediaeval craftsmanship has escaped the attention of iconociasts, and has acquired through the centuries a lovely sheen, more entrancing than the finest paintwork.

It was dark within the church when I began my drawing, but soon the sun burst through. I was able now to discern in the shadows above the loft that the whole semi-circle was timber filled, and that the cross has survived. So here in this remote Monmouthshire village, we have what in my experience is unique, a pre-Reformation screen, loft, and cross. On each side of the cross three openings surmounted by tracery enabled watchers in the loft to see the ceremonies at the altar.

Bettws Newydd — the pre-Reformation screen, rood loft and cross.

The loft is reached by stone steps made in the thickness of the south wall. Although not of Herculean build I had to edge myself up the steps, as I used to beat to windward in our yacht.

I have found that the surest way to appreciate a work of art is to sketch it. In sketching the extremely complicated rood-loft at Bettws Newydd I discovered that the 14 framed sections, none alike, contain in their bases one quatrefoil and two trefoils each. Above these, in superb and varied detail, arise sweetly from the ogee arches a series of fanciful floral or foliated devices. Above these is a trail of leaves such as William Morris loved to use in his wallpapers four centuries later, and,below, a trail of vine-leaves and grapes. Beneath all this, yet in harmony with it, the screen is like a pair of delicately framed windows with a doorway in the centre, the slender uprights holding trefoil tracery surmounted by sets of three lights.

Enfolding this treasure, the white walls and cradle-roof are the perfect foil, and when the western sunlight pours in and diffuses, the effect is of over-whelming grace, sanctity and praise, as if the ancient craftsman with the Benedictine before him had chanted as he worked.

"O all ye Green Things upon the Earth,

bless ye the Lord; praise him and magnify

Him for ever."

While the church is, of course the special treasure of Bettws, the hamlet at the crossroads has its interest. Motorists who drive through, and even those who halt for refreshment at the inn, are apt to miss a sight which takes us back in imagination to those days when the Norman conquerors were raising their strongpoints throughout our land.

The Inn and Norman mound, Bettws Newydd.

Alongside the old road which runs almost due north from under Usk Castle we have still Norman mounds at Beech Hill, one near Trostrey church, and many more beyond Bettws Newydd.

At the crossroads an excellent example comes into view, as shown in my sketch. Known locally as "the Brake." It is a tree-clad height rising to 318 feet, with the flat circular summit typical on such "mottes." The view from the top is impressive and shows how the artificially raised hillock commanded not only the north-south road, but also the road from Raglan to the Usk crossing.

The **Black Bear** at **Bettws Newydd** is a study in black and white. Its sign must be one of the best-known in the land, standing comparison with the "Monmouth Cap" at the Llangua and the "White Hart" at Caldicot. in spite of its well-cared for appearance the inn is at least 200 years old.

From the village I drove onto Clytha hill and a walk across a windswept hilltop field took me into the hilltop camp where all was calm. Now National Trust property (for Captain Geoffrey Crawshay presented it in 1945), **Coed-y-bwnydd** charms all visitors — except one, who, I understand, is repelled by some sinister influence which she encounters there. Maybe she is allergic to aristocracy, for the old Welsh name signifies *"the wood of the gentry."*

The trenches of Coed-y- bwnydd prehistoric hill fort.

In summer the undergrowth prevents exploration, but on this afternoon I could see how the fort had been planned, one trench only guarding the precipitous west and north-west, but two, three or four trenches on the other sides. The shape was roughly oval, the entrance guarded by a tumulus, the circumference some 500 yards and the extent about eight acres.

I know few viewpoints more thrilling than the north-west edge of Coed-y-bwnyyd. On a clear day, Blorenge, the Black Mountains, Sugar Loaf, Skirrid and Graig are dramatic points on the skyline, the middle distance is green and pastoral, the fruit blossom forming white pools among the green, the brown churches and white farms peep out from among their trees, while our exquisite river steals out of Breconshire and meanders across towards us, takes a look at the Clytha hills, and then slips sweetly past Llanfair Kilgeddin and away.

When our friend Archdeacon Coxe saw the fort in 1800 he recorded that the tumulus at the eastern entrance appeared to have been fortified at each extremity with towers, of which the foundations were still visible.

He found many stones scattered on the tops and sides of the ramparts, and concluded *"The character is British, but the strait roads exhibiting vestiges of paved causeways diverging from it in all directions, favour a conjecture that it was once occupied by the Romans."*

From Coed-y-bwnydd we descend Clytha Hill to reach the A40 and turn left towards Abergavenny. After about 4 miles turn left for The Bryn, otherwise known as Llangattock-nigh-Usk.

Nigh the river, not the town, which is over six miles downstream, **Llangattock** is one of the many churches dedicated to the saintly Cadoc, son of our own St. Gwynllyw (St. Woollos). To find it, I took the turning marked "Bryn" near the King of Prussia on the Abergavenny-Raglan road.

From the barn I walked along "lavender lane" until the cross of its ancient base, and the church with its pyramidal roofed tower confronted me. In that tower, which used to hold four bells, one only remains, but that bell, with the two at Redwick and the Undy bell, is of particular interest, for the four were made at Bristol in the fourteenth century and were brought to Monmouthshire about 1380. The inscription on the Llangattock bell reads:

SANCTA THOMAS HORA
PRO NOBIS

The church of Llangattock-nigh-Usk.

On my drawing of the church tower two large and two small niches are shown in the east wall. Two similar niches, also empty, are to be seen in the east wall of the church, and though unusual they may have held effigies of saints, all facing east.

Surrounded by daffodils, I studied the ancient building. Bradney suggests that St. Cadoc's was founded in the sixth or seventh century, and the present structure, stripped now of its ivy, bears a charming time-honoured appearance. Roof-marks on the east wall of the tower show that, of old, the roof of the nave was taller and had a steeper pitch.

In the churchyard, near the porch, I found the interesting tomb shown in the smaller sketch. At the head stands the "kneeling-stone," in which the knees would fit while prayers were made for the soul of the departed. I cleared away much grass and turf to lay bare the inscriptions "Vive Ut

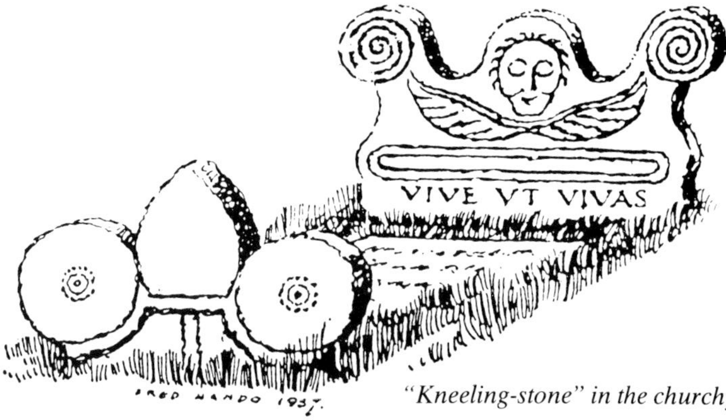

"Kneeling-stone" in the churchyard.

Vivas" (Live so that you may live) on the kneeling-stone, and on the flat stone recording the burial of John Howell of Llanwenarth in 1774, followed by the quatrain:

No life so long but
Sickness may at tenit
No life so strong but
Death at last will end it.

Within the church I noted the stairs and doors which led once to the rood-loft but nothing now separates nave from chancel!

The splendid little brass showing the lady with the sonorous christian name "*Zirophaenzia*" hangs on the chancel wall. The memorial slabs — one showing the rector in 1644, a front view of head and body, but side views of his feet — are quaint, and the Norman font and Beauchamp titles (William Beauchamp was Lord of Abergavenny in 1392) should not be missed.

Close to the font is the massive slab known as the memorial stone of "*David the Warrior.*" Though much worn, the interfaced cross, the axe and part of the inscription are still visible. A century ago Mr. Wakeman read the inscription as "*David ap Ieuan Lloyd*": fifty years ago Bradney and Hobson Matthews gave the reading "*David ap Hoell*": in good light I could decipher only the word "*David*" prefixed by a cross.

The stone dates probably from the mid-fifteenth century, in which event David the Warrior would perhaps have been among the Welsh contingent at Banbury in 1459, fighting for the Yorkists.

In a glass case near the font is the greatly treasured Welsh bible — Y Bibl Cyssegr — printed in 1620. It was the second edition of the translation made by Bishop William Morgan of Llandaff in 1588 and it is engaging to imagine Drake and his fellows chasing the Spaniards around our island while the little Welsh bishop sat in his quiet room at Llandaff re-writing the bible in Eden's language.

This copy was bought by the rector, the Rev Francis Lewis, for twenty shillings in 1769. From that date its story is not known until Mr. William Haines of the Bryn bought it in 1889. On his death in 1922 Mrs. Haines presented it to the church.

Mr. Haines was a much loved man of Gwent. Deeply concerned in most county affairs, proud of his English and Welsh ancestry, an authority on his county's history, he built up a unique collection of books on Monmouthshire and his library is now enshrined as the Haines Collection in the borough library at Newport where it is in constant use by students and general readers.

By the Horse and Jockey turn left and follow a short road to join the A4042 and then turn left for the village of Llanelen.

Llanelen church.

Beautiful as its name is the setting of this village **(Llanelen)**. Dark, almost black, evergreen trees guard the church, the woods behind sleep in their robes of gold and russet, scarlet and apricot, and towering above all suave, silvery in the morning mist, the mountain stands as if in benediction.

Memories of such beauty brought tears to the eyes and ache to the hearts, of Llanelen men exiled overseas in wartime.

The church is dedicated to St. Helen — not, as many believe the saint who was mother of Constantine the Great, though she too was a native of Britain, but Helen, daughter of Eudaf of Ewyas. She married Magnus Clemens Maximus, Emperor in Britain Gaul and Spain from A.D.383 to 388 and the confusion has arisen because they also had a son named Constantine.

Old inhabitants aver that there was once a peal of bells in the church tower. Of the present couple, one, inscribed *Lewis Llewllyn: John Phillip Edward. Anno 1662* was recast in 1922 and hangs above the older bell which is inscribed *R O Ienkin Richard William Watkins Smith 16* — two further examples of the insistence on immortality of the churchwardens at the end ofCromwell's regime and the beginning of the new reign.

These bells have been housed for the last thirty years in an extraordinary spirelet which with its pinnacles and crockets has impressed some writers as elegant, but is actually out of scale and harmony with this simple village church.

Strolling around the church, I noted the projection which contains the stairs to the vanished rood-loft, some ancient windows retained during the rebuilding, and everywhere signs of loving care which showed that St. Helen's church still holds a warm place in the hearts of the village folk.

Within the church the same care was evident and among ancient relics preserved is the original font which at some time must have been used outside as a sun-dial.

The village blacksmith, Llanelen.

Down in the village, under the spreading chestnut tree, I met the village blacksmith — a mighty man, with a halo of silver curly hair. As we stood watching the cars flashing past towards Abergavenny or Llanover, he commented, "I wonder if they realise that the road here is hollow. The cellars of the old Hanbury still exist under the road."

Llanelen, I gathered, had three inns — the "Hanbury," the "Lion" and the "Butchers' Arms." Lady Llanover converted the Hanbury into a temperance house which she named "Y Seren Gobaith" — "The Star of Hope" — and closed the other two taverns.

Long before the days of her ladyship there were "great doings" at Llanelen "up in the Punchbowl," and he pointed to the mountain. "Cromwell's men were encamped, and when the Royalists came a great battle took place, and do you know?" — in a low voice — "when we were digging a grave in the churchyard some years back we found, 18 inches beneath the surface, ten skulls — four here, three here, two here, and one there, in the form of a square — all reminders of that battle."

At Llanelen House adjoining the churchyard, lived from 1840 onwards *Sir Thomas Phillips, who had been mayor of Newport in 1839 and was knighted for the part he played in repelling the Chartists. In later years he wrote the charming biography of James Davies, the saintly schoolmaster of Devauden, and attended on Sundays the services in Welsh, at Llanelen church.

"From his house," said the blacksmith, "a secret passage leads to Castell Pridydd and Abergavenny Castle, and another to Llanover and Coldbrook" — which seemed somewhat extended, even in this county where secret passages are of abnormal length!

*** F.J.H. omitted to mention that the grave of Sir Thomas Phillips is in the corner of the churchyard. It is surrounded byiron railings. — Editor.**

Continue along the A4042 to reach Llanover.

In spite of the injunction to go slow, the motorist travels through **Llanover** at too great a speed to spare a glance right or left. Yet Llanover, either the "model village" on the main road or the ancient secluded hamlet on the river bank, is well worthy of a visit.

Surely no more delectable countryside could be imagined. Against a background of mountains the colours of which change from moment to moment like shot silk, embossomed among the noblest trees in the country, and threaded by one of the fairest reaches of the Usk, this green land called for men's best efforts in converting it into a site for a village.

"The Old Duke" inn, now the "Gwesty Dirwestol" temperance house, Llanover.

How pleasant — how unusually pleasant — it is to record that in the riverside hamlet, the park, and the model village, the church and the chapel, the great houses and the cottages reach a standard in their design and materials rivalling the best in Cotswold architecture. What is equally important, the interior planning of Llanover homes displays knowledge of the needs of the housewife, and provides the spaciousness and comfort to gracious living.

What set this high standard? Lady Llanover, who was born at Llanover House must have visited many of the ancient homes of Gwent and admired the brown roofs and the ashlar walls, the chimneys, the windows, the porches.

Gwenffrwd — the white rushing stream — deserves its lovely name. As it tumbles into Llanover it gives character and sweetness to the glen. I imagined the ford before the present road was made. "*Rhyd-y-Meirch*," it was of old, and as I stood over the waters, I could almost hear the stamp of the stallions.

Gwenffrwd Wool Mill, Llanover, with the snow-clad Sugar Loaf in the distance.

From its source, 1,350 feet up the silver stream dashes down to turn the wheel of the Gwenffrwd wool mill, and thence the wheel of the Ryd-y-Meirch corngist mill — both now silent. To find this mill, take the first left turning past the post office. The great wheel is now silent, but the mill in its romantic setting is very beautiful. A tablet on the wall does not help us to date the building. How old, then, is Rhyd-y-Meirch Mill?.

In 1826 the manor and estate were sold to Mr. Benjamin Hall (later Lord Llanover). Included among the buildings of the estate was "*the water corn-grist mill at Rhyd-y-Meirch recently erected working two pairs of stones.*" It is therefore safe to assume that the water wheel turned the stones for 130 years.

A short walk from Rhyd-y-Meirch Mill took me to the old brown-roofed house which was once "*The Old Duke*" *Inn*, but which is now "Gwesty Dirwestol" — the temperance hotel. "*The Old Duke*" was one of seven inns on the estate, but under the influence of Lady Llanover, who was a fervent teetotaller, all except one disappeared, and that one rejoices in the name of the "*Goose and Cuckoo.*"

To find this tavern you must journey upwards for nearly two miles above the village. As far as I can determine, the seven inns were the "*Nag's Head,*" now the post office, the "*Old Duke,*" the "*Goose and Cuckoo,*" the "*Oak*" and the "*Seren Gobaith*" (Star of Hope) at Llanelen, the "*Nightingale*" at Pen Croes Oped, and the "*Grey Goat.*"

"The Old Duke," now the *"Gwesty,"* was, I assume, the Duke of Wellington. My sketch shows part of the house as seen from the main road. In the background at the left are the shadowed slopes of Mynydd Garn Clochdy, 1,470 feet high from which the lovely brook has cascaded.

The "Mari Llwyd" Inn sign at Llanover post office.

Opposite Porth-y-Pentre (village-gate) at Llanover is the post office marked *"Llythyrdy"* — literally the *"letter-house."* Although so near The Old Duke, this was another of the village inns, Penceiffel! — The Nag's Head. Above the entrance is an extraordinary canvas, painted over a century ago, which was the inn sign.

Under a crescent moon a weird procession approaches Llanover House. In the foreground a young man leads a white-draped figure with a horse's head, followed by other men, dimly seen. Fortunately the picture is glazed, so the colours are still good.

As far as I know, this inn sign is our only coloured illustration of the Welsh custom known as the Mari Llwyd (or Lwyd). At Llanover where Welsh culture in all its forms was fosterd, the Mari was produced at every Yuletide, but the last of the celebrants died some ten years back, and the *"Venerable Mary"* (if that is what is implied) is now but a memory.

To reach Old Llanover turn left just past the Llanover Post Office and after a mile turn left again and within ¾ mile you will come to Llanover Church.

The cool sunlight of a March morning silvers **Old Llanover**. Set against the backcloth of clouds and great hills, church and cottages dream. The church glows between a vast yew tree on the one side and a weeping willow and lone pine on the other. A sparkling nant-y-mynydd joins the Usk under the arch of Ty'r Afon, the fishing-cottage. Muted jade-green the river flows strongly.

In this soft mystic light, the lovely hamlet seems too ethereal for this bustling, go-getting age. Can it survive? With all the slighting and despoiling of beautiful places, what can be done to retain this other-world sweetness of Llanover? We can schedule ancient monuments and places of historical significance. Before the horrid thing known as "development" deposits petrol-pumps and road houses in this shrine of ours, will some enlightened authority take appropriate action?

Less than eight years ago, Old Llanover was in danger from thc mightiest form of vandalism. It was actually proposed to erect an enormous generating power station, covering 180 acres of rich agricultural land, and to raise four cooling towers, 200 feet high, and four chimneys, 300 feet high, in this vale of tranquillity.

Old Lanover.

The vandals misjudged the men and women of Gwent. Led by that redoubtable ancient Briton, Mr. D.L. Jones, O.B.E., our forces met the invaders in full strength, and after a series of battles our sacred soil was saved.

As I stood on the river bank on this bright morning, my imagination reeled at the thought of Llanover shadowed by a pall of smoke, and the exquisite river poisoned and ruined by the wastes of industry. The battles fought for Llanover and Machen Vale are among our finest gifts to posterity.

Built by my dear old friend, the late Henry Smith, the pretty suspension bridge enabled Mr. Leslie Pim, M.P. — greatly-beloved Mr. Pim, to whom all the country folk took their troubles — to visit the old church.

In the churchyard lies buried the lady who gave character to Llanover, who restored the ancient arts and crafts of Wales to their rightful level, who reintroduced the joys of beauty into country life. Lady Llanover was escorted to her grave by twenty maidens dressed in Welsh costume, and on her coffin lay a wreath of white roses sent by the Duchess of Teck, who was to become in years later Queen Mary.

Inside the church are inscriptions which, as Coxe pointed out in 1800, are clear evidence of the Welshman's pride in his lineage. William Prichard and Matthew Prichard, father and son *"of Llanover, Esq.,"* are commemorated, *"linealy descended from the Bodye of Cradocke Vraich vras Earle of Hereford and Prince between Wye and Seaverne."* A proud claim this, for Cradock was a knight of King Arthur's Round Table!

Return to the A4042 and go straight across to follow the back road leading over the canal and below the slopes of Mynydd Garn Wen to reach Mamhilad.

St. Illtyd's church, Mamhilad.

Dreadful happenings occurred thirteen centuries ago at **Mamhilad**. From Llancarfan in Glamorgan a procesion of monks brought the body of St. Cadoc in a golden coffin; when they arrived at Mamhilad they were attacked by Danish pirates.

A hundred of the pirates attempted to lift the coffin and failed. In fierce anger the chieftain smote the coffin with a stout stick whereupon it bellowed like a bull and an earthquake shook the valley. Now thoroughly frightened the Danes retreated, but one returned, and cut off a golden pinnacle with his hatchet. The pinnacle fell into his lap and *"burned him like fire,"* so he replaced it, and the pinnacle adhered as if by gold soldering.

His friends watching him from afar were now horrified to see the miscreant melt like wax before a fire. They returned whence they came, and had no further desire to plunder our land or lay waste the holy places.

The stile into the churchyard is a tombstone inscribed:

Heare lieth the
body of Aron Moris
deceased the 25th day
of May 1680

The churchyard is notable for its yew trees, one of which is very old, while another holds its place in the churchyard wall, In the foreground of my sketch is the cross, which though modern is raised on an ancient chamfered base. There are two porches, and the strange quatre-foil window above the western porch masks, I believe, an Early English window partly hidden by the musicians' gallery. This gallery by the way, reached by steep steps from the nave, has an ornate front decorated with oak leaves and acorns, which may have been transfered from the rood-loft. Standing in the centre at the west end one notes that here again is an example of chancel deviation to the south, seen through the semi-circular chancel arch.

Sir Joseph Bradney tells us that before the wooden floor was laid on the chancel floor he noted a sepulchral slab incised with the figures of a man and woman wearing ruffs, and above them three small crowned figures.

Mamhilad church is held with St. Michael's, Llanfihangel Pontymoile. Thirty years ago last month, the Reverend Christopher Cook, vicar, died, aged 102. He had served both churches from 1855 to 1925, but had not preached in Welsh since 1860.

How the dear old vicar — and the bishop — used to chuckle over the former's response when the bishop suggested that at 95 the vicar might consider retirement: "Had I known that it was not to be a permanency I should never have accepted the post." He had been vicar then for seventy years!

A perennial topic of talk in the Mamhilad countryside is the **Roman Road**. In one of my articles I suggested that this ancient trackway which certainly swings up and down from Llanhilleth through Pontnewynydd and Trevethin to Mamhilad did not end there, but continued eastwards. Every farmer in the district confirms my theory, and it is quite fascinating to hear how the plough turns up the stones of the old road. "Traces of paving" are marked on maps of the district, but unfortunately the paving near the tithe barn and near Troedyrhiw is covered by the tarmac of the roads.

Troedyrhiw from Persondy, Mamhilad. The Roman road climbs the hill on the right.

"Troed-y-Rhiw" signifies *"the foot of the rise."* To find it I turned left at the Star inn at Mamhilad and continued along the Roman Road until the white farm buildings shone ahead. Driving slowly (for I had not travelled the old road for thirty years) I came at length to "the foot of the rise," and left the car.

In order to reach the 'Roman' road leave your car at Mamhilad and walk up the turning by The Star for about ¾ mile and look out for the ancient trackway emerging from the trees on the right.

The Roman Road, Mamhilad.

Dark, steep, mysterious the hollow way climbed between its tall banks. Good cobbles of an average size of 6in by 4in filled convexly the space between bigger stones lining the ditches. Water poured down the ditches and across the cobbles at the foot of the rise into a road-side ditch, but none poured down the cobbles.

As I climbed the track on this still, mild afternoon, the quiet of the hillside, the scent of my tobacco and the solitude had a hypnotic effect on me. It was the old spell which I have known for so long. Spirits of the past floated around me. I saw the road-makers, the shepherds, the foresters; I saw the Elizabethan priest from Persondy visiting the fine new houses in the parish: I saw the "navigators" cutting the canal, I saw — yes, my dreams vanished as I saw in the twilight of this canopied lane a campion in full pink bloom glowing up at me from the shadows. Did campions I wonder, grow on the banks of the Roman road as the legions passed that way?

I drove on the short distance to **Troedrhiw farm**, where I met Mr. and Mrs. Joseph Williams, senior, Mr. and Mrs. Joseph Williams junior and their two bright children. Here, as elsewhere in Mamhilad, I was assured that the track of the old road was known east of Mamhilad along the line of Tredomen, near Pentwyn towards Pandy Pool below Chainbridge.

And then, like a good showman, young Mr. Williams produced a little coin which he had dug up in his garden. It was a Roman coin and has since been identified by Mr. Cefni Barnet as of c270 A.D., bearing on the obverse "IMP.C. TETRICUS. P.F. AVG" around the crowned head and on the reverse "PAX VG" around the figure of Pax.

Continue from Mamhilad to rejoin the A4042 near I.C.I. Fibres. Turn right with care and shortly on the left will be seen the Waun-y-Clair inn.

The Waun-y-Clair inn Llanfihangel Pontymoile.

There is something about the **Waun-y-Clair** which combines the quaintness of yesterday with the comfort of today. A long white house with its own pull-in (which was the narrow old road), it is the port-of-call for hundreds of motorists, including commuters, those strange products of this age who find satisfaction in living leagues away from their work.

The name is a problem, *"Waun, waen,"* is a meadow. *"Clair"* may imply a fly, for *"Cleren Lwyd"* is a horse-fly or gadfly, and "claren las" is a bluebottle. Yet who would wish to name a meadow after gadflies or bluebottles? Was there only one meadow so infested?

More attractive is the second clue. "Cler" were itinerant minstrels, who may have found this site a popular halting ground. The chances, however, favour the theory that the meadow was one of the many parcels of land belonging to the Clares, that famous family whom we have come across at Usk and Tintern, and whose shield of arms may be seen in Glamorgan, in the cellar of the Tredegar Arms at Newport and in a famous Cambridge college.

A century back the inn stood alongside the narrow little main road, opposite a fine house named Maesderwen. That house is now the Woodlands and from its beautiful grounds I sketched the Waun-y-Clair.

Clothing the gentle hills behind the inn are woods named Coed-ty-mawr, Coed-cae Wat, and Coed-Bryn-Tovey. At the foot of the hills winds the romantic Berthin brook which for centuries turned the great wheel at Little Mill.

Horse and Jockey Inn, Llanfihangel Pontymoile.

A mile further on is another inn at Llanfihangel Pontymoile and the adjoining church.

While many of our visitors regard Tintern or Raglan as the symbol of our county, others tell me that when they close their eyes in afterdays and think of Monmouthshire, a memory of a pub and a church flashes before them — the thatched inn and the cream-washed church at Llanfihangel-Pontymoile.

There is a tradition in the district that the inn is 765 years old. This does not surprise me in these days when geo-chronologists can date the earth, but a few questions elicited the belief that the inn and the church were built at the same time.

There is regrettably no evidence which would date the founding of the church in 1192, and the present inn — there may have been an older house which has left no trace — cannot be of much earlier date than 1600.

But as I sat at a big fire in the bar and thawed my frozen fingers (for sketching on the Jockey pitch on a windy, frosty day tends towards refrigeration) a great comfort, age-old and soul warming, wrapped me around.

When the inn (which, by the way, was of old the "Horse and Groom") was a remote posting inn on the coach road, the only water supply was the well which though now covered, may still be seen on the forecourt.

In the bar is an attractive old oil painting of *"Honest Tom,"* a famous trotter ridden by Billy Fletcher, of the *"Horse and Jockey,"* for its owner, John Williams, who kept the *"Star"* at Mamhilad.

Seen from the porch of the Horse and Jockey the church of **St. Michael** is very beautifully placed against the shadows and muted tints of the hillside. Its dedication marks it as one of the few llanfihangels on low grounds, for St. Michael — as in Cornwall and across the Channel at Mont St. Michael — is generally a hilltop saint.

I entered the church from the vestry and noticed at once that the steps up into the pulpit spring from the vestry. A single central corbel above the chancel arch is possibly the only relic of the rood loft which may have been reached by a continuance of these steps.

Church of St. Michael, Llanfihangel — Pontymoile.

A modern painted image of St. Michael stands above this corbel and draws attention to the impoverished geometry displayed by the architect who designed the chancel arch. Work of finer character is seen in the eastern Perpendicular window, and everywhere throughout the church are signs of the care bestowed by the parishoners of today.

I walked along the nave under the barrel-roof to inspect the arches at the west end. At Llangovan the masonry supporting the bell turret was massive in the extreme; here at St. Michael's the supporting arches are full of grace.

From Llanfihangel Pontymoile follow the dual carriageway to turn right at the roundabout opposite the Crematorium to reach Croesyceiliog.

The Upper Cock Inn, Croesyceiliog 1965.

The name **Croes-y-Ceiliog** delights and dismays the visitor. Welsh scholars, insist that the spelling should be *"Ceilog,"* but *"Ceiliog"* has dug itself in. You may hear of an enormous stone sculpture of a cockerel; you may learn that the reference was to the "cock-horse" which was removed at the hostelry after the coach had climbed the hill.

Some local authorities aver that the Upper Cock Inn was given its name because of the cock-fights which took place in the inn-yard. But I prefer to place Croesyceiliog with all our other place-names based on birds, and trees, and streams, on hills and valleys.

When I was young the sign of the *"Upper Cock"* bore this charming Welsh invitation:

"Dyma dafarn Croey y Ceiliog
Groesaw i bob un am ei geiniog,
Cwrw da i bawb trwy dalu,
Dewch i mewn, chwi gewch ei brofi."

"Here is an inn — the Cross of the Cock —
A welcome is yours, for a penny,
For payment so small, good beer waits you all,
come in, taste our ale, good as any."

In English:

In spite of the decreased purchasing power of the penny I beg the proprietors to replace the Welsh stanza on their inn sign.

Four months before the advent of the Chartists in July 1839, a baby girl was born to the wife of the inn-keeper of the Upper Cock. I met that same baby girl when she was a silver-haired lady of 84, living in a cottage in Pontrhydyrun.

"Oh, yes," she said, in reply to my question. "I was living at the inn when they came in, but" — with a twinkle — "I don't remember much about their visit. My parents used to tell me how they all demanded drinks and called on all the men to join their ranks."

It is salutary to remind ourselves that these men marching on Newport were prepared to give their lives in support of a charter which demanded "six points."

1. — Universal suffrage.
2. — Equal electoral districts.
3. — Annual Parliaments.
4. — Vote by ballot.
5. — Abolition of the property qualification.
6. — Payment of M.P.s.

Drive past County Hall and turn right (with care) onto the A4042 dual carriageway and then left to follow the B4236 back to Caerleon, passing through Llanfrechfa and Ponthir on the way

Dedicated to All Saints, **Llanfrechfa church**, with the exception of the south porch and the impressive tower, was rebuilt in 1873. One glance at the west wall of the nave showed that the old church was considerably lower; the ancient timbers in the porch are still sound, and amidst the modern glories of the big chancel, with its reredos of the Last Supper, its sedilia, and its screen with figures of Our Lord, St. Mary and St. John, I was interested to find the original piscina in its primitive simplicity.

At the far end of the north aisle I found the baptistry, where if desired, the ordnance of baptism by immersion may be performed. My small drawings are of shields on the front of the baptistry, decorated with the ark, the fish, and the Chi-Ro monogram — this last recalling the secret sign on the lamp discovered at Caerleon two years ago by the late Dr. Nash-Williams.

The embattled tower bears on the south a sundial, on its western face a stone carved with part of a Maltese cross, and another with an O.S. bench mark.

The church of All Saints, Llanfrechfa.

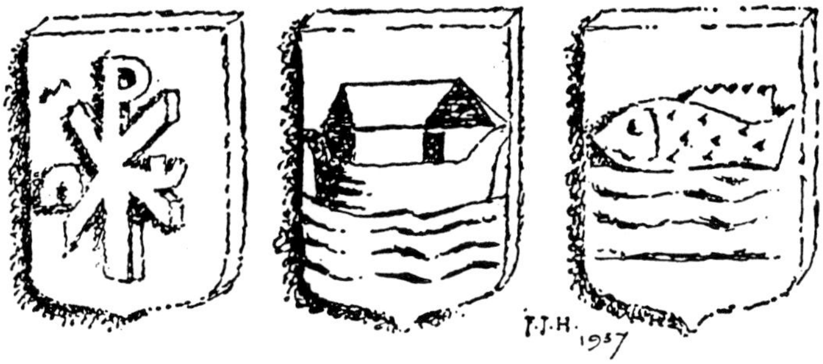

Carved shields on the baptistery.

The **Ponthir House** is a famous old hostelry in the village of Long Bridge ("pont hir"). In the garden at the rear are the old stables, retaining still their cobbled floors and horse-troughs, while the inn itself, though modernised, has much to remind us that it was erected, as the inscription shows, in 1710. The excellent new roof replaced the stone roof, over which, according to a local legend, a noted highwayman rode his horse for a wager.

Ponthir House 1953.

EDITOR'S NOTES

The major change in the Vale of Usk since Fred Hando was roaming this quiet valley has been the construction of a concrete highway (A466) which now provides a fast but scenic route for the motorist passing beneath the wooded escarpment of Kemeys Graig and the solitude has given way to the noise of fast moving traffic.

Fascinating finds have been made in recent years at Bulmoor where excavations have revealed a Roman settlement of some importance. At Kemeys Manor, Fred would be pleased to see that the stone portrait of George Kemeys has now been taken indoors for safety and is mounted on the wall above one of the old fireplaces. Below the house, beside the river the little church of Kemeys Inferior is just a sad overgrown pile of stones; a now forgotten and rarely visited site.

Excavations have also taken place recently near Trostrey church by the Gwent Antiquarian Society who have revealed the site of a large mediaeval building.

At Bettws Newydd the hill fort of Coed-y-bwnydd may be visited on a circular walk which starts from the National Trust picnic site at Clytha and a visit in May is recommended for then the summit of the fort may be seen thickly covered in bluebells.

The village blacksmith at Llanelen has long since gone and his forge is now a craft shop selling a wide range of souvenirs etc., to passing visitors. The mills at Llanover no longer operate and Rhyd-y-Meirch has been turned into an attractive house. High on the hillside the elusive Goose and Cuckoo is still the only pub at Llanover but the route has now been waymarked making it easier for the stranger to find his way there.

At Mamhilad the so-called Roman road is generally regarded today as a Mediaeval pack-horse route and its surface has sadly been damaged by the selfish activities of motorcyclists but it still provides a magical route for the walker heading up to the ridge above.

The Waun-y-Clair, The Horse and Jockey and Ponthir House through modernisation have perhaps lost some of the old quaintness but they still serve beer and offer a warm welcome to passing travellers who come this way.

CHAPTER THREE

Twyn Barllwm.

Wandering in West Gwent

Twyn Barllwm — Risca — Cwmfelinfach — Gelligroes — Cwrt-y-Bella — Aberbeeg — Crumlin — Abercarn.

Twyn Barllwm is the southern climax of a ridge — Mynydd Maen — which stretches from Pontypool to Risca. The great tumulus at the summit, 1,374 feet high, may present problems to the archaeologist, but as boys we were taught that it contains the bones of a prehistoric British chieftain.

The modern student laughs at our gullibility and teaches his children that the Normans built the great mound in order to give them control over the Western Valley!

Sons and daughters of Gwent, can you imagine our ancestors at Risca being cowed by a battalion of cloud-cuckoos a mile away? And such a mile!

Normans forsooth! Look at the view. You gaze to the south over Uskmouth, the Severn and Somerset. Return, and pick out the sapphire jewel which is Pant-yr-Eos. Can you make out the Holms and the Monkstone, and Penarth head?

See how many of the heights of Glamorgan and Gwent, swimming in a golden sea of light, are known to you. Rest your eyes now among the silver mists of the Carn Valley. Then explore the great hills of Brecknockshire and Herefordshire and Gloucestershire, to come to rest again on our own Wentwood and the Vale of Usk. And can you arrange for your shadow to fall on Christchurch tower?

When you have taken your fill of views, slip down the tump and walk along the green ridgeway northwards.

Stark and forbidding on a March morning: green and inviting in June; an upland paradise of blazing glory, its bracken flesh-pink beneath an October sun; or white in its winter cloak, Twyn Barllwm is always impressive. Its lure at sunset, however is compelling.

The ridge of Twyn Barllwm/Mynydd Maen may be viewed from Ridgeway at Allt-yr-yn on the north-west side of Newport. To reach the summit of Twyn Barllwm follow a narrow lane from High Cross to a point directly below the mound which can then be reached by a 10-15 minute walk. Alternatively it may be ascended from a car park on the Cwmcarn Scenic Drive.

I find charm in imagining the village of **Risca** in 1852. Built around its lovely old church, Risca had become a parish in 1839 and there is evidence that as early as 1291 among the chapels attached to the great mother church of Bassaleg was Risca. You will find much of the story of Risca church with its extraordinary vicissitudes in the writings of Canon E.T. Davies, whose "brief history" in the centenary booklet of 1953 integrates the building, the history, the clergy and the people into a community where tremendous changes — e.g. there were but 2,744 inhabitants a century ago — and incredible industrial development have still at their centre the church of St. Mary.

St. Mary's, Risca, before its demolition (from a print of 1852).

Appropriately in this county, the church had as its neighbours two inns — The Bell and The Yew Tree. I understand that John Walker, proprietor of the Yew Tree, parish clerk, sexton, collected his clientele whom with himself he locked in the church during that November night in 1839 when the Chartists were marching towards Newport.

My drawing is a reproduction in line of a charming wash-drawing made in 1852 just before the old church was demolished. During the demolition it was observed that among the fine ashlar of the walls were Roman bricks and lumps of concrete.

Four years before the demolition Mr. D. Rhys Stephen of Newport had written, "Few know that while the name Isca has perished in connexion with Caerleon it is still used every day as the name of the little parish and village between Maesaleg and Mynyddislwyn and its very heart is situated at the foot of Twmbarlwm. 'Isca' with the Welsh definite article 'Yr' constitutes the present name of the parish."

When the demolition took place and the village lost its picturesque saddle-back tower careful note was made by Wakeman of the contents of the gable on either side of the tower:

"On either side were stone cists containing bones, in one instance with twenty or thirty beads of jet or Cannel coal. These receptables were 4ft. by 2ft. and 4ft. above the floor — too small to receive a body at full length."

The main thrill, however, occurred when the foundations for the chancel of the new church were being laid. Here, six feet below the level of the old church a wall forming part of a circle of some twelve feet radius had obviously enclosed an apartment still paved with Roman tiles marked with "LEG. II. AUG" so familiar on the relics of the legionary fortress. In familiar style too was the embedding in concrete 18in. deep and a base of flag stones with their lower edges embedded in the concrete.

What was this apartment above which the worshippers of St. Mary's kneel to make their communion? When one remembers the earliest churches built by the Normans with their semi-circular eastern apses — St. Peter's in the Tower, St. Margaret's in Edinburgh castle, and a score more — one is tempted to imagine an early Roman church at Risca.

Follow the A467 via Risca to Crosskeys and then take the A4048 to reach Cwmfelinfach where the turning to Babell Chapel is signposted.

In my days the old folk pronounced the name *"Rishca,"* just as they called a coppice a *"coppish."* They had their dialectical tricks of referring to the *"reservoy"* and *"the hool point,"* and when the good man returned home unusually late he found his Sar'ann "tamping mad."

"The folklore of Risca is rich and exciting. We have the Devil's Apron-strings on Machen heights, and when I was young me blood raced as an old son of Risca pointed to the mountain ridge, purple against an orange sky. "At times," he chanted, "I have seen a figure striding along that ridge. He had leather trews, a pointed hat, a pointed beard, a belted skirt. Whether Roman or Phoenecian I could not be sure!"

Buttressed by two stalwart Welshman I entered the Valley of the Little Mill — **Cwmfelinfach**. You will remember how Archdeacon Coxe in search of Swiss scenes in the wilds of Monmouthshire, came to the Vale of "Sorwy" (Sirhowy).

"The features of this vale are more wild and romantic than those of the Ebbwy; it is narrower and deeper; and the shelving declevities, laid out in meadows, stretch to the edge of the torrent, which roars in a profound abyss, obscured by overhanging trees."

"Sorwy" is a compound of two ancient water-words, found also in the Sor Brook and the River Wye. With the exercise of some imagination we were able to recreate from The Sirhowy Valley of to-day, the Sorwy Valley of Coxe's days, but in this process we had to remove the products of industry, the nineteenth and twentieth century domestic and church architecture, and the black precipitate from the stream.

The "frightful grey tip," which disfigures the countryside of Islwyn, poet of Gwent.

We turned left at the village of Cwmfelinfach and made for the Calvinistic shrine, the spiritual home, the tabernacle in the wilderness — "*Babell.*" I had been warned of a shock, but the first view of the little Bethel was fearful, devastating.

Babell, small and pathetic, was overshadowed by a grey monster, mountain-high, which, in its sinister progress up the valley, had covered four football pitches and one cricket field, and seemed, from our viewpoint, poised like some hideous mammoth ready to crush the House of God.

Never in my journeys through these valleys have I felt, as I felt at Babell, the horrid impact of the wastes of industry on the shrines of beauty and goodness.

Islwyn the sweet singer of Sirhowy, sleeps in the God's-acre of Babell. We stood before his monument, utterly unable to recapture his sweetness and light, restless in mind and soul by reason of the frightful grey tip, down which, in maddening regularity, fell the contents of the ariel buckets. And this has continued, night and day, for forty years and more. The grand men of the valley, after garnering the harvest of the mines below, came to the surface to find their "*wild and romantic vale*", their "*crystal stream,*" and their sanctuaries desecrated by the grim tip.

Shaken by the sight and sound, we entered the chapel. The elders talked to us of their beloved Islwyn; they showed us the bardic chair which he had won at Rhyl Eisteddfod in 1870 for his poem "Y Nos" (the night). The sound of the conveyor buckets followed us into the quiet chapel.

They told us how they were struggling to keep aflame the torch of Christ in the Valley of the Little Mill. "We have but small congregations and no resident pastor. We depend on visiting lay-preachers and we are getting old. Few of the young ones are here to follow us, and when we go..."

The buckets tipped, tipped...

Said Phillip ap Afanfryn to me, "Sit here, maestro, and play the organ while we sing Islwyn's hymns."

In a moment, the place was transformed. Even I, who know little Welsh, was constrained to sing, and led by Phil's magnificent baritone, the eight of us sang to the glory of God in the heaven inspired words of the valley-poet, composed on Snowdon above the clouds:

"Gwel uchlaw cymylan amser.... „
"See above life's clouds and shadows
See, my soul, the Land of Light,
Where the breeze is ever balmy,
Where the sky is ever bright,
Blessed myriads
Now enjoy its perfect peace."

Banal and thin is the sound of the English translation after the thunder and glory of the massive Welsh words, sung to 'Bryn Calfaria.' Then we sang "*O arwain fi i'th nefol ffyrdd,*" and half-a-dozen more, until our souls burned within us.

The conveyor-buckets were still tipping as we emerged into the evening light, but they had lost their sinister power. The spirit of the gentle poet-pastor, living on in his deathless hymns, had at naught the onslaught of ugliness, and fixed our minds on the Land of Light.

We strolled down past the tip to Pont Lawrence where the little river comes hurtling through a single arch. Here, where the great hill rises tree-clad almost to its summit, Islwyn must have brooded in his terrible grief when exactly a century ago, his life was shattered by the death of Ann Bowen, a tragedy which produced his greatest poem, "Y Storm."

About a quarter of a mile upstream from Pont Lawrence was the Little Mill which gave its name to the valley. At the back of the Mill, Mr. George Morgan tells me, was a large pond where members of Twyngwyn Church were baptised by immersion.

My enterprising guide, Douglas ap Arthur took us now through Ynysddu (the black island) and along the Old Road to **Gelligroes** (the sunken cross-road — possibly a ford). Here we discovered a pretty hamlet of stone built cottages, another single-arched bridge, and an ancient over-shot water-wheel working a flour-mill. In a house in the hamlet shown on the left of the sketch, many of Islwyn's Welsh poems were first printed. His poem. "*The Nightingale*" was composed in the lane near Gelligroes.

The miller, as ingenious as he was kindly, showed us the millstones, "adjusted to one-thirty-second of an inch," the mechanism connecting the wheel with the stones, and his own device by which the wheel generated sufficient electricity to light his mill and to charge many a battery.

Gelligroes Mill

It was at Gelligroes Mill that some of the earliest wireless experiments in Gwent were made. The miller's brother and the farmer at Ty Llwyd over Ynysddu were in communication in 1908, and our miller remembers orders for feeding stuffs being received "over the air" before the First World War.

The inner casing of the roof of the mill consists of some of the old box-seats from Bedwellty Church. We spent a gay half-hour tracing the names scratched on the panels — among them "*Sarah Jones and Joseph Jones of New Tredegar.*" Near the mill in the old days was an inn, now disused, prettily styled "The Woodman's Delight."

Our tour of the valley was followed by visits to delightful old people who gave me memories and legends of their beloved Islwyn. The youngest of nine children of Ty'r Agent, Ynysddu, in 1832. Ty'r Agent (the "*Old Machine House*") is no more, but Greenmeadow and Ty'r Glyn, later homes of the poet, survive.

He went to schools at Tredegar, Newport and Cowbridge, and to a college in Swansea. It was at Swansea that he fell in love with Ann Bowen, the beautiful girl who inspired his early poems, and whose death in 1853 clouded his life — a tragedy which produced his greatest poem, "Y Storm."

Later he married Martha Davies, of Swansea, and they came to live at Ty'r Glyn. Martha was ideally suited to tend the highly-strung, sensitive poet, and her loving sympathy and devotion are remembered in the valley to this day.

"What do you recall of Islwyn as a man?" I asked Mrs. Walters, aged 92, of Glenside.

Islwyn

Mrs. Walters, aged 92, of Gelligroes.

She thought in silence for half-a-minute, and then murmured, "He was well-liked. He was witty. He was nervous after dark, but while he was still alive we knew him to be a great man.

"On one dark night Islwyn was visiting a cottage a short distance from his home. When the time came to return, the two girls of the cottage accompanied him, lighting his way with a candle. Suddenly his servant jumped out from behind a bush and for a joke, blew out the candle. Frightened beyond measure, Islwyn ran back to the cottage, quite sure that the light had been extinguished by a dead lady who 'walked' that lane.

"Islwyn," she continued, "kept a bantam cockerel indoors as a pet. To amuse the children, of whom he was very fond, he would request the bird to sing, whereupon it would crow."

Little by little, from Mrs. Walters and Mr. George Morgan (aged 90) and others I was able to paint a mental picture of Islwyn. I see him as a short, slight man, with brown eyes and hair, a broad calm brow and a gentle voice and manner. Childless, yet loving chilren, loving also his home and his dear wife, he was one with his people, who revered him.

Like many other sensitive souls, he found solace in a pipe of tobacco, and frequently in two, for while he smoked one, he filled another. He played a harmonium. He was Secretary to the Ynysddu School Board. Maybe tobacco was a heaven-sent sedative following these activities.

Ty'r Glyn — Islwyn's House, Ynysddu.

Though I cannot read his greatest poems, I am convinced that Islwyn's short life — for he died at forty-six — was filled by an art devoted to the highest. His love for his people, like his love for his Master, brought the angels from heaven to Cwmfelin, and my short visit to the Valley convinced me that the influence of those angels, like the influence of Islwyn, remains strong and sweet.

Gelligroes Mill is off the A4048 just south of Pontllanfraith. Cwrt y Bella church site is at Gwrhay to the north of Oakdale off the B4261 which may then be followed to Crumlin to see the site of the great viaduct that once spanned this valley. Turn left here along the new road to reach Aberbeeg where the packhorse bridge may be seen. Return via Crumlin and Abercarn to perhaps visit the Cwmcarn Scenic Drive and Visitor Centre.

From the heights above Tredegar the Sirhowy has tumbled and frothed its way down to Cwm Argoed. During the ages it has cut its way so that the western bank is precipitous, the eastern gentle. But what of its extraordinary name?

It seems clear that "*Sirhowy*" is a modern corruption of its old name "Sorwy", made up of two water-words, "*Sor*" and "*Wy,*" which Arthur Machen insisted were older than Welsh or Anglo Saxon and were brought here by the Celts in their journey west-wards from the "Land of Spring."

"It was a diverted stream from the Sirhowy which turned the wheel of your mill," I suggested to a lady of the village. Standing alongside me as I sketched she corrected me. "No, a stream dashed down the slope then alongside the houses to the mill-wheel. All the buildings were concerned with the business of the flannel factory, and their deeds are dated 1902."

My mind went back to the other great "flannen" factories which I had visited at Machen, Maesycwmmer and Llanover. "Early and late, by candle and lamplight and daylight the men and women laboured at their spinning and weaving, dyeing and sewing." — that was at Machen, where "Weavers' Row" still survives. I am sure that similar busy days were known in the seven or eight buildings of the Cwm Argoed Welsh flannel factory.

The dyes used were red and grey. I hold the theory that a red-flannel curtain separated Wales from England. At the approach of winter every mother in Wales cut and hemmed squares of red flannel and sewed tapes at the two top corners ready to fix on the chests of her little ones at the first sign of a cold.

But the flannel had to be RED. Dear old George Morgan of Ynysddu, who had seen and helped with the dyeing of the flannel at Argoed gave me the reason for the unfailing efficacy of the red flannel. Wild Welsh mountain ponies would not drag the secret out of me.

Cwrt-y-Bella church

I crossed the Sirhowy bridge and drove up to the **Cwrt-y-Bella church**. The name implies the court of the wolf, but I suspect that Sir Thomas Phillips transferred the name from the old farmhouse in Newport near the end of the Sirhowy tram-road.

The part played by Sir Thomas as mayor of Newport when the Chartists attacked the Westgate hotel has obscured the kindly, helpful side of his character.

As owner of the Gwrhay mines he was disturbed by the ignorance and squalor of the district and built the Cwrt-y-Bella school and school-house, paying for the buildings, garden, equipment and master's salary. Unfortunately subsidence rendered the school ruinous, but the schoolhouse still stands.

In addition to the school Sir Thomas made himself largely responsible for the erection of Cwrt-y-Bella church. Building materials were hauled up Hall's tramway whence the men and women of the valley took them up to the site; one Mari Shams (James) is still named as the heroine of this project. "She carried twice as many slates on her head as any man, averring that she had no money, but could serve God in that way."

The church was completed in 1857 and dedicated to Saints Phillip and James — the surname of Sir Thomas and his wife's maiden name.

For many years the services were conducted in Welsh, and its famous vicar, the Rev. Rees Jones (who gave the name to the Parson's Bridge) used to drive his trap from his home in Blackwood, walking thence to the church where he spent his Sundays, fortified by sandwiches made by his wife and pots of tea from one or other of the cottages.

While generally in good condition the church needs a certain amount of repair to forestall more serious trouble.

The Colliers Arms, Gwrhay.
("The Pick and Shovel")

At the **Colliers' Arms** ("the Pick and Shovel") Mrs. Margaret Carpenter told how until 1955 the inn had been but a cider and beer house, both drawn "from the wood." She took me across the forecourt and showed me the corroded rails of the tram road which had come down alongside Nant Gwrhay. One section of rail found recently bore still the initials B.H. implying that Benjamin Hall, later Lord Llanover, had been active in the construction of the tram road.

It was the Sirhowy rail road, the earliest in Wales, of which the Grwhay line was a branch, that brought the load of coal to Newport so vividly portrayed in the splendid painting which we have allowed to go to Cardiff. Painted by John Thomas in 1821 it shows the four horses pulling the "drams" of coal past Cwrt-y-Bella Farm on Cardiff Road, with top-hatted Mr. Samuel Homfray sitting on the first dram and the masts and spars of ships in the distance.

Ancient bridge in Aberbeeg.

My drawing, believe it or not, is of a pack-horse bridge in the centre of **Aberbeeg**. Its parapets are replaced by bricks and it is cluttered up with a mass of impedimenta which I have not included.

There it was discovered by my old friend Ali, who promptly collected me and drove me to inspect his find. As we stood admiring its graceful lines, we removed from our minds the surrounding excrescences, and saw the bridge spanning the crystal Ebbw Fach, while the sturdy figure of "Edmund Jones the Tranch" crossed on his homeward way. Later again as we climbed the grand hill and turned south to Oakdale, Penmaen and Pontllanfraith we seemed to be following the footsteps of the prophet as he went about our hills and vales doing good.

Before 1853 **Crumlin** was a secluded hamlet comprising a few miners' cottages, The Navigation Inn and the Company's shop. "Navigation" implied the construction of the canal, the labourers being the "navvies."

Pontypool lay 4½ miles away, Newport 12 miles, and at this point it was proposed to make an intersection of the "Western Valleys Railway of the Monmouthshire Railway and Canal Company" and the "Taff Vale Extension of the Newport, Abergavenny and Hereford Railway."

The cost of building large masonry piers at a height of over 200 feet above the valley was staggering. Several engineers submitted designs for an iron viaduct, but it was Thomas William Kennard whose work caught the fancy of the judges.

Crumlin Viaduct.

His scheme was to use open cross-braced pillars to support the 1,500 feet of super-structure; the heaviest piece of ironwork would weigh less than a ton and could be drawn up by a common windless, sheer legs and pulleys.

One iron pier would be completed in ten weeks, while a masonry pier of the same dimensions as many months; the pressure on the foundations of Mr. Kennard's iron piers was less than one fifth of that exerted by a stone pier. Each pier consisted of 14 columns, of which two only were vertical. All the others converged at an inclination of about 1 in 12, and while I am no engineer I find it absorbing to note the extreme care taken over every detail of construction, the confidence in the cross-braced pier construction — the first of its kind — the calculation (confirmed in use) of the strains on the girders, and the clever arrangements made to permit the expansion due to variation in temperature.

I cite as an outstanding example of this variation the records dated February 12, 1861, and August 27 in the same year when the temperatures of the girders varied from 32 degrees Fahrenheit to 98 degrees, and the length of the girders increased by 2¾ inches.

The deflection of the girders caused by a passing fully-loaded train was ⅝ inch and the girders returned to their exact form immediately the train has passed.

Those items were but a few of the myriads noted. When I stood on the top road leading towards Abertillery and looked down on the graceful structure I got the impression of an enormous "harp of the winds" and wondered idly if any engineer had calculated the vibration frequency of the strings.

On December 8, 1853, Lady Isabella Fitzmaurice inserted into a recess in the stonework (of the foundations of the first pier) a cup containing coins of 1853, the permanent bolts were fixed, a bottle of wine was broken, and the work of erecting the pier — still called the Isabella pier — began. That cup with its coins is worthy of preservation. The cost of the viaduct was £62,000; the cost of the Britania Bridge, twenty feet longer, over the Menai Straits, was £601,865.

On Whit Monday, in 1857, after many severe tests, the viaduct was opened. Excursion trains ran from all parts of the kingdom. The centre of the viaduct was spanned by a floral arch, from which great banners hung bearing the inscriptions, *"Long Life and Prosperity to T.W. Kennard," and "Long Life to the firm of Kennard Brothers."*

Cannon were placed on both sides of the valley from which volleys were fired "with slight intermission throughout the day, causing the mountains to reverberate with their thunder."

Soon this splendid and beautiful viaduct will be but a memory. History, we know, is the record of "makes and breaks," an era of construction followed by an era of consolidation, then an era of destruction.

Abercarn church.

In 1853 Sir Benjamin Hall gave **Abercarn** a Welsh Anglican church. It was to serve the needs of the Welsh speaking Anglicans, but when a dispute arose with the vicar of Mynyddislwyn, who wished to introduce one English service weekly, Sir Benjamin transferred the building and its parsonage (and the Capel Cae Celynen) in 1862 to the Welsh Calvinistic Methodists.

All that I gathered from the writings of Rex Pugh ("Glimpses of West Gwent") and the enthusiastic young Vicar of St. Luke's Abercarn, but until last March I had never seen "*Eglwys Gymraeg, Abercarn*"; then I had a glimpse of its picturesque lines from the vicarage garden. In company with the vicar — the Rev. David Brunning — I journeyed up the tree lined drive to the west facade of the church.

Over the porch I read the stone inscription A B H 1853, indicating that the church was the joint gift of husband and wife. The impressive western gallery bore the arms, in full colour, of Queen Victoria and of Benjamin and Augusta Hall.

Twenty-seven pews suggested that congregations of more than 200 were expected; the handsome three-decker pulpit was surmounted by a brass commemorating Lord Llanover, and this, like all the other inscriptions was in Welsh.

I should record that the stonework throughout, the timbers of roof and pews and pulpit, the delicate tracery of the windows, bear tribute to the loving care bestowed on this beautiful sanctuary. Its memory will remain with me as of a gem securely set in upland sylvan serenity.

They tell at Abercarn of a great occasion when Thomas Griffiths, the blind harpist of Llanover, went to Abercarn to give a harp recital. He was met at the station by Prince, the local harpist, who had lost the sight of one eye, and who proceeded to carry the harp of the distinguished visitor. As they were approaching a level crossing Prince took the blind harpist's arm, urging him to walk with care. "Is it not strange," he queried, "that a harpist with one eye should be leading another harpist with none?"

"Have you got but one eye, Prince?" shouted the great man. "Give me my..... harp!"

EDITOR's NOTE

Twyn Barllwm still holds its magic and dominates the skyline above Newport and the surrounding area. The legends of this mystical mound are still quoted and its origin argued. In recent years restoration work has been carried out on the mound by a team of men working on a Manpower Services Commission Scheme in conjunction with Gwent County Council. Countless feet and illegal motorcycling activities had caused severe erosion to the mound over the years. A flight of steps now provides an easier ascent to the top which has been raised in height and re-turfed and the base of the mound has been surrounded by a low fence. The project won a Prince of Wales award in 1986.

At Cwmfelinfach the massive tip has been removed and Babell chapel has been restored as a memorial to the poet Islwyn. It also serves as an exhibition and information centre for the Sirhowy Valley Country Park where picnic sites, walking routes and other facilities have been established for the enjoyment of visitors and locals alike.

At the time of writing the mill at Gelligroes is still in operation but Cwrt-y-Bella church is no more, having been demolished over a decade ago and judging by Fred Hando's comment it was obviously in a poor state when he paid a visit.

The old packhorse bridge at Aberbeeg has survived despite new road construction and building demolition at Aberbeeg but sadly Crumlin Viaduct is now just a fading memory having been demolished in 1966. Just before it was taken down, it featured in a film called Arabesque, starring Gregory Peck and Sophia Loren.

Abercarn is now visited by people on their way to the nearby scenic drive at Cwmcarn where the Forestry Commission operate a seven mile route which enables the motorist to drive high up into the Ebbw Forest to enjoy extensive views, picnic sites, forest and mountain walks. At the entrance to the drive is a visitor centre provided by Islwyn Borough Council.

CHAPTER FOUR

Land of the Trilateral Castles

Llanvetherine — White Castle — Llantilio Crosseny — Rockfield — Llangattock-vibon-Avel — Newcastle — Skenfrith — Grosmont — Campston Hill — Llantilio Pertholey.

To reach Llanvetherine follow the B4521 from Abergavenny and then turn right about 2 miles further on where a signpost indicates the way to Whitecastle.

Cruising lazily along the Ross-Abergavenny road, I saw an interesting church tower. The upper portion of the tower was wider than the lower part, being supported on corbels.

Bright April sunshine flooded church and churchyard, inn and farmsteads. The village was **Llanvetherine**, midway between Cross Ash and Abergavenny. '

Lovers of the church had brought the brightest gifts from their gardens in readiness for the Sabbath. Daffodils, primroses and fruit blossom expressed the ecstasy of springtime, but four of the window-sills in the nave were filled with red, white and blue anemones — a floral prayer for the Queen in her coronation year. I absorbed their glory as I stood at the entrance.

Then I realised that near me was a presence. Leaning against the wall of the porch was a big stone slab on which was carved the figure of a saint with upstretched arm. This was St. Gwetherine, to whom the church was dedicated, and after lying for many years untended in the churchyard the slab had been brought into the shelter of the porch.

I noted the northern deflection of the chancel. I read many of the interesting memorial inscriptions. Then suddenly I was confronted with two extraordinary stone portraits, resting against the east wall of the chancel.

Rev. David Powell.

The Rev. David Powell, Vicar of Llanvetherine, who died in 1621, is shown on the right-hand side. His head rests on a cushion: he holds a Bible. His cloak, edged with a decoration of oak leaves and acorns, is thrown open to display a tunic, with knotted belt and knee breeches with no "bombast." Fine as these clothes were, they lapse into insignificance beneath the splendour of the vicar's facila embellishments.

A moustache of noble proportions, hoisted well above his upper lip, sweeps thence to his ears. Pendant from the lower lip is a special beard, well ordered, covering with fair precision, the shapely chin. The beard proper, believe it or not, is disposed in five plaits, each of which reaches to and emphasises the line of the collar. Surely such a cleric, high-perched in his three-decker pulpit, began his ministrations with such notable personal advantages that none of our clean-shaven parsons could hope to equal.

The Rev. David Powell, could he be brought to us in all his glamour, would fill St. Paul's with enthusiastic congregations, and incidentally would substitute for the sad uniformity of the masculine visage some of the charming variety of a more spacious and leisured age. What would I give for instance, to see my friend Alderman..... complete with a handlebar moustache and a five-plait beard?

Mistress Powell — the vicar's wife.

The vicar's wife whose effigy stands to the left of the pulpit, is a figure of womanly grace and sweet piety. Some miscreant has carved the date, "*22 of April 1715,*" on the stone but Mistress Powell's three tiered ruff enables us to accept the two figures as contemporary.

Between the candles rises from her shapely head the high-crowned hat which should make Llanvetherine a port of call for every student of Welsh costume. The ring on the second finger of her right hand reminds us that until 1549 the wedding ring was worn on the fourth finger of the right hand.

The sculptor has solved the difficult problem of the front view of the lady's feet by giving a side view. His rendering of the vicar's feet is more successful.

I cannot hope to do justice to all the treasures of this country church, but I must describe the carving on the oak tablet fixed on the west wall of the nave. As my sketch shows, the "five wounds" of our Saviour are shown, and among them are "The Instruments of the Passion" — the dice, coins, hammer and scourge — all rendered with a loving touch and a child-like simplicity.

Out in the sunshine again, I asked my way to Caggle Street, I found it around the bend to the east of the village — a steep 'street' climbing the hill, it seemed to nowhere. "Could you tell me," I asked a lady of Caggle Street, "the meaning of Caggle?"

"Oh, yes," — with a smile — "'Caggle' means 'dirty,' 'stony' and so it was when it was the Roman road leading from White Castle to the Skirrid."

From her flower-filled garden I got a good view of White Castle, and from the top of Caggle Street an imposing prospect of the mile long ridge of the Skirrid.

White Castle — Castell Gwyn — stands in lonely majesty south of the Abergavenny-Ross road, and from many of the viewpoints around it presents a study in splendid isolation.

The name *"White Castle"* has not been satisfactorily explained. Colour names, such as Castell Glas (green) and Castell Coch (red) are given to other castles in ancient Gwent. Some writers argue that Castell Gwyn was once whitewashed and point to fragments of whitened cement which survive but a Castell Gwyn existed before the present stone castle arose. The name is probably connected with Gwyn (white) the owner of the castle at the time of the Conquest, whose brothers, Bach and Aeddan, were lords of Skenfrith and Grosmont.

Gwyn's primitive fortress was in all likelihood of wood. Even this was not the first fortification on this site, for earthworks were raised here at a very early date and in my opinion may be named with those at Llantilio Crosseny as of Bronze Age.

Gwyn takes his place high among the heroes of Wales. When he was old and blind his castle was beseiged and captured by a Norman invader. The fierce old Welsh chieftain complained bitterly to King William Rufus and demanded that he and the Norman should fight in a closed and darkened room. The Red King's sporting instincts were aroused. The request was granted, and in the terrible duel that followed Gwyn won, and his castle was restored to him.

The present building is of the early or middle thirteenth century. To the student it is of extreme interest, as it is perhaps the most valuable example of the transition stage between the 'motte and bailey" and the 'concentric" castle. The first concentric castle built in this country by the Normans was raised at Caerphilly in 1267. Compared with Caerphilly, White Castle is primitive, for there is no evidence of accommodation for the garrison, who may have lived in wooden shelters.

Yet White Castle has all the charms of a story-book fortress. The walls follow the line of the prehistoric mound, and their colour and curves are reflected on the surface of a deep moat. The entrance is across a bridge and under an archway between two towers. If the original mound was raised for sighting purposes, the erection of these towers gave still wider horizon, and the view from the top of the right-hand tower baffles description.

Down in the moat you may see two giant carp, followed at times by thousands of their miniature gold-sparks of offspring, but venture not too near, for the wild blood of the ancient Welsh swans fills the veins of the present swan-custodian of the moat, and with a guttural Cymric swan-oath he will be at you!

The strength of this fortress was a tribute from the Normans to their Welsh foes. An outpost against such enemies needed to be strong, for Gerald (who died about 1220 A.D.) tells that the arrow of the Welsh bowmen pierced the oak door of Abergavenny Castle, which door was four fingers thick; that their arrows passed through the armour-protected thigh of a Norman rider and mortally wounded his horse.

Continue along the same road to drop down to join the B4233 near Llantilio Crossenny. Hen Cwrt is at the junction of the two roads. A footpath from here also leads across the fields to the church and village.

In this village the folk still talk of **Llantilio Crosseny**.. *"Llanteilo"* it should be, for the beautiful church on the hill commemorates Saint Teilo.

Saint Teilo, Bishop of Llandaff in the sixth century, was the son of Saint Tegfedd to whom, the lovely old church of Llandegfedd was dedicated.

When the Saxons attacked this district, Iddon, sore oppressed, sought assistance from the godly Teilo whom he found praying on the mount "in the middle of Cressinic" and prayed fervently while Iddon and his men fought and defeated the invaders.

The king gave the mount and the land around it to the saint and it is therefore fitting that the church dedicated to Teilo should stand on the hillock where the saint prayed.

As my sketch shows, Llantilio — a "city built upon a hill,, — cannot be hidden. The graceful spire on the central tower, like the spires of Grosmont, Ross and Monmouth forms a landmark for miles around and gives character to the park-like countryside.

Llantilio Crosseny.

One Sunday we sat in a meadow above the "moat" (where the battle took place) and listened to the bells of Llantilio. Of these bells, five are inscribed with prayers for the church and Queen Anne, and the sixth dated 1821, with a prayer for the church, and for "peace and good neighbourhood."

As we sat and listened, the ringer played the old hymns of our childhood, and their music combined with the tinkle of the brook and the bird-song to induce a sense of peace which also recalled child-hood Sabbaths.

Stone Corbel Head at Llantilio.

Peace reigned within the grey church. Tall perpendicular arches replace the early English nave arcade, although the lancet windows survive at the ends of the aisles. The chancel is of the decorated period.

While the south transept is original, the north transept has been replaced by the Cillwch Chapel, separated from the chancel by three arches. From the chapel the view of the high altar is obtained through one of two "squints".

To left and right of the east window are very interesting stone corbel heads, one of which I have sketched. The mode of the hair-dressing dates these as of the reign of Edward II (1307-1327).

The north wall window near the pulpit recalls Sir David Gam of Llantilio Crosseny who won immortal fame at Agincourt, and whose home, Hengwrt, stood in the "moat".

The flat stones in the chancel are of great interest. Two of the stones show costumes of Stuart days, and the third in memory of Vicar Owen Rogers who died in 1660, bears three candles ten angels' faces, and a quaint inscription.

The inn at Llantilio Crosseny bears an ancient name — **"The Hostrey"**. There was a tenement called "Le Hostry" in the village, but on a different site, in 1459. Very picturesque is the scene when the foxhounds meet in the open space before the inn.

"The Hostrey," Llantilio Crosseny.

We then paid a return visit to Cillwch, one of the most interesting ancient houses in northern Gwent. To my delight, Cillwch has been restored to something of its former splendour, and the owners have now a beautiful home, every room furnished with taste.

It was very satisfying to find that the ancient window portraying St. George and the Dragon, which had been removed, has been replaced. On another window I read the signature of the glazier who had inserted a pane on *"31 July 1853"* — a century ago this month!

In the attic we opened a small door in an inner wall at floor level, crept inwards and peered down into a secret room six feet square. Cillwch was a Catholic home in the days of the Oates Terror, and with the Vicar of Llantilio so fanatical in his hatred of the Catholic priests, it must have been essential to have a hiding place near at hand. Yet the entrance to this small room has not been discovered; it was certainly not effected from the attic.

We inspected the unicorn and the pelican plaster decorations, the carving on the ornate fire-place, the linen-fold panelling inthe dining-room, and the great beam-bolt, four inches square used for fastening the front door. Robert was interested in the working of this beam, but far more interested in a friendly old English sheepdog.

At the junction of the Monmouth and White Castle roads in Llantilio is an impressive square moat enclosing an acre of ground. Traditionally this was the site of Sir David Gam's house and as I stood there I recalled the village legend that if Davy Gam's children held hands they would stretch from **Hengwrt** (his *"old court"*) to the church, a quarter of a mile away on its mound.

The moated site and the church of Llantilio Crossenny.

Though I prefer the apocalyptic tradition and legend, I must record that after thorough excavation The Ministry of Works reported that the moated site in the South West corner of the deer park was occupied in the thirteenth and fourteenth centuries, possibly by a manor house belonging to the Bishops of Llandaff *"who had held land in Llantilio from the earliest times"*.

Sir David Gam, hero of Agincourt, was probably not here, but in the fifteenth century his son-in-law Sir William ap Thomas or the latter's son formed a deer park here which continued until the destruction of Raglan Castle.

It is held by many scholars that Shakespeare's Fluellen was based on Dafydd ap Llewellyn, otherwise David Gam, who with his son-in-law Roger Vaughan of Tretower was knighted for valour on the field of Agincourt, 1415.

It was this same David Gam, who on the eve of the battle was asked by the king for the strength of the eneny. His reply, as recorded by Raleigh in his *History of the World,* is typical of this terse, tough man: *"Enough to be slain, enough to be taken prisoner, and enough to run away"*.

Sir William ap Thomas's wife Gwladys, daughter of Sir David Gam, and widow of Sir Roger Vaughan, the other knighted hero of Agincourt, has come down to us as *"the Star of Abergavenny, the strength and support of Gwent and Brychan"*. Among their descendants were the Dukes of Beaufort and the Vaughans of Tretower.

In the north wall of that noble church of Llantilio is the window of Sir David Gam, installed there during this century. In the shield are the three Vaughan children's heads with necks couped and entwined by serpents; the three spearheads and chevron represents Sir David's descent from Maenarch, who was fourteenth in descent from Caradawg, one of the knights of King Arthur's Round Table.

This inscription reads:

DAV GAM EQV AVR DOM
LLANTILIO CROSSENNY
OCCISUS IN CAMPO AGIN-
COURT ANo. 1415.

The name "Gam" has been preserved through the centuries by family names such as Games, Gamsan, Gamlin. Theophilus Jones notes that the great family which once owned the whole county of Brecknock was represented in his day by "*one Games, the common bellman of Brecon.*"

Continue along the B4233 to reach a junction with the B4347 where you turn left for Rockfield.

St. Cenedion's Church, Rockfield.

What a soothing sight for a townsman's tired eyes! Embosomed by hillside trees, an exquisite church with timbered tower adds its beauty of holiness to the white cottages, the widespread green, and the Monnow.

A grand setting for a cricket match, some would say. Perfect for residential flats, money-grubbing developers would croak. Fifty, sixty, 65, records the speedometer as the motorcyclist flashes along the riverside road.

Of course, every motorist drives through — I repeat, through — **Rockfield**. Can I persuade him, I wonder, to "rest beside the weary road, and hear the angels sing?"

In a graceful meander the Monnow has curved from old Perth-hir to greet the village. I parked my car near the cottages on the green and walked alongside the river while it talks to me of Craswall and Longtown, of Cloddock and Alltyrynys, of Grosmont and Skenfrith. Still charged with the mountain oxygen of the Hatterralls, it dances its way to Abermynwy and the Severn.

I took the church lane. Near the lych-gate I paused, charmed by the Benedictine inscription under the archway of the well. "O ye Wells, bless ye the Lord." From the churchyard the cottages on the green, under their guardian trees, seem like an illustration in a Beatrix Potter fantasy.

I stood and viewed over the churchyard cross and the clipped yews, the church of Rockfield, dedicated to St. Cenedlon. This saint with the tuneful name, lived 15 centuries ago, with 48 brothers and sisters in the ancestral home of their father, Brychan. Strange it is to think of one of the girls — our own Gwladys — snatched from Bronllys by the wild pirate-prince Gwynllyw, and of this other, Cenedlon setting up her cell here, near the well of Rockfield. And did not Gwaldys live in a cell near the Lady's Well at Pont Ebbw?

Nave, porch and chancel at St. Cenedlon's are reconstructions, but the tower and its superstructure are original. Up in the wooden lantern are three bells, with the following inscriptions:
1. Memento Mori, Januar 9, 1655; 2. Soli Deo Detur Gloria, Januar 9, 1655; 3. Feare God, Robbat Upton, Jon Williams, churchwardens, 1669, I.P.

Unusual it is to find ecclesiastical activity in 1655! Elsewhere in our land donors and churchwardens seem to have come out of hibernation only when the Merry Monarch appeared in 1660!

With its massive masonry, timbers, louvres and lancets, this tower is the south-eastern link in a chain of handsome structures which stretches up into mid-Wales, and includes primitive Cwmyoy and assured Skenfrith.

Within the church I found the font in the tower room, a location unusual, but not unique in our county. The ancient font survives on the floor of the north aisle, which is separated from the nave by a three-bay arcade.

Under the communion table is a stone slab six feet long. A long Latin inscription on it commemorates the Rev. Matthew Prichard who died in 1750, and was the priest at Perthir, the venerable home of the Powells and the Lorimers. The priest officiated in Perth-hir chapel, which was dedicated to St. Catherine, the patron saint of Monmouth Girl's School.

The boys of Monmouth School will be interested to learn that in1795 the vicar of Rockfield, the Rev. Thomas Hughes, was usher at their school, while in later years another vicar, the Rev. George Monnington, was headmaster.

In the north aisle are windows portraying the saints Christopher, Athanasius, Matthais, Nicholas, Dubricius and Ceceilia, each with an appropriate symbol.

And when I returned the church key to the Scottish owners of the adjacent house I saw an artist's dream — garden flowers of June, a perfect lawn, and the stonehouse designed not merely for comfort, but also to add beauty to a beautiful setting.

Continue along the B4347 and turn left after about 2 miles and then take a right turn for ½ mile. Park and walk down a lane to reach Llangattock-vibon-Avel church.

Seemingly buried in a coppice of tall trees we espied the red pyramidal roof of a church tower **(Llangattock-vibon-Avel).** Up high on the left loomed a vast house. My son Robert counted 29 chimneys, and when a lady of Llangattock instructed us that this imposing dwelling had its own staterooms and was originally designed as a dower-house to the Hendre, we were suitably impressed.

Yet it was the church with the red roof that attracted us. From the far end of the big churchyard, the view was of a hillside sanctuary stereoscoped against massive trees and accompanied by a well-designed memorial cross in granite.

Three-light Tudor windows were a later addition to a tower designed obviously for defence. While I was sketching, Robert essayed to climb the ladder to inspect the bells but had to forgo that pleasure because of the frail ladder. Instead he explored the memorials within.

The church and cross, Llangattock-vibon-Avel.

This remote country church was one of nine churches in our county dedicated to St. Cadoc, son of Gwynllyw. My readers will remember the Rockfield church dedication is to St. Cenedlon, aunt of St. Cadoc. Both these churches were among the gifts made by Withenock of Monmouth to the monks of St. Florence to maintain the priory at Monmouth, and the manor house above Llangattock church was built on the site of a grange of the same priory.

The Evans' memorials in the church recall the great family who lived for centuries in the old manor house. Thomas and John Evans then "ap Ievan," were of Llangattock and lived there before 1600, while an interesting brass on the south wall of the church commemorates *"Thomas Evans of Llangattacke-Vibon-Avil."* who died in 1629.

"Hee liveing, loucing and belov'd, now dead,
Of all lamented is; His wife her Head
Rich lost their loue, the poore their life, his spirit
Left, here his corps; and heaven doth inherit."

Sonorous Latin inscriptions are to later members of the same family.

The family associated above others with the church and countryside is the Rolls family of the Hendre. On the south side of the chancel is the Rolls chapel, and their memorials are to be found in the chancel and a south window. The rebuilding of the church, except the tower, in 1875 was undertaken by the family; their tombs are between the church and the manor.

Of the Rolls memorials I noted especially those to Lord Llangattock, killed in the battle of the Somme, and Charles Stewart Rolls, "pioneer of motoring and aviation, killed flying at Bournemouth, July, 1910," whose statue graces Agincourt Square in Monmouth.

Robert had discovered a Welsh inscription on a porch memorial, which was to James Water, A.D. 1690 and read:
"Gweddin bawb ar y Jesu hwn ddyc on yn hawdd... a dangos ynni gwir olevni pryd dde y gwiwion yn gweli. W.H."

The memorial to Alice Evans who died in 1706.

The translation, I am told, presents difficulties. I shall be glad if a Welsh expert will enlighten me on this, as well as on the extraordinary *"Vibon Avel"* attached to the church name Llangattock.

My smaller illustration is copied from the memorial stone to Alice Evans who died in 1706. It shows how a Monmouthshire monmumental mason portrayed an angel, complete with wings, fleurs-de-lis and other emblems.

Continue along the B4347 to reach Newcastle. Castell Meirch, Newcastle.

Behind the farm house **(at Newcastle)** rises a tall tump, tree clad. Here was Castell Meirch (the Castle of the Stallion) used, so Bradney assumes, as a Norman outpost of Monmouth Castle. Part of the moat remains filled with water, but on the summit of the mound we found to our horror, a large concrete tank. Our comments in English and Welsh had best remain unrecorded, but I find it difficult to imagine the barbaric ignorance which would permit such a crime. Here, on the heights, with noble views of our old land in every direction with over a thousand years of history beneath it, a concrete tank! As soon, I should have thought, erect a galvanised iron roof over Stonehenge.

Like Twyn Tudor at Mynyddislwyn, this tump was peopled with many a spirit, and these folk had relatives in the parish. Some of the relatives, fierce female tree-dwellers, lived in an extraordinary oak tree. When Archdeacon Coxe visited Newcastle in 1800, he was much impressed by this venerable relic, one of the largest branches of which, broken off in a violent storm, had yielded fifteen cart-loads of firewood.

The Newcastle Oak in 1800

The hamadryads of The Newcastle Oak wielded imperious powers. One villager breaking off a bough, broke his arm; another fractured his leg; and when the last branches fell in a great gale the cottagers who used any of the wood in their fireplaces set their cottages alight. My sketch, copied from Coxe's *History of Monmouthsire*, shows the tree as it was in 1800.

Other relatives of the tump sprites were less anti-social. They acted as attendant spirits of the seven springs and the wishing well, and while the springs cured rheumatism, the well granted their wishes to the maidens who threw pins into its water.

Yet another spirit lived in the well inside the Castle Farmhouse. Before this well was covered over, an old lady had seen on several occasions a ghost rising from the depths of the well.

It was not to view any of these items that we had climbed to Newcastle. Like many other Monmouthsire folk, we have tried each year to see the three famous flowering trees of our county — the Handkerchief tree of Mounton, the Judas tree of Moyne's Court (now, alas no more) and the Wistaria of Newcastle. I was anxious to see the effect of the blizzards on the Wistaria.

The Wellington Arms Newcastle.

Acknowledged by botanists to be the oldest and most remarkable of all Wistarias, it was, until a few years back, a very beautiful ornament to the ancient inn. Until 1815 this hostelry was the King's Head, but when Colonel Evans returned from Waterloo he had the name changed to the Wellington Arms. The Wistaria was then a century and a half old. In other words, this Wistaria was planted, as Mr. Piddington of Monmouth School reminds us, long before the birth of Caspar Wistar in whose honour the genus was named.

When I knew it first, the trunk was five feet in girth and at its bifurcation was sealed annually with concrete. Branches led left along the inn and stable walls, and right along the walls of the courtroom for the inn was once used for the petty sessions.

Great nails driven into the walls to support it, were imbedded and known locally as *"ingrowing nails."* Stout oak brackets were added and this magnificent shrub in mid-May, along the whole of its one hundred and fifty feet, was draped with pendant flower clusters, soft in outline, hazy in mauve hue, their fragrance drifting over the hamlet.

With sadness I record that our Wistaria displays but a shadow of its former glory. Bravely it has struggled again into meagre leafage and blossom, and it may yet, with a succession of warm summers and mild winters, recover completely. Maybe the water-sprites and tree-nymphs of Newcastle will take a hand in its rehabilitation.

A delectable destination from any direction is **Skenfrith**. Come down to it across the rich red lands from Ross; climb out of Monmouth to Newcastle and descend that shadowed pitch; take the magnificent way from Llantilio Crosseny via White Castle; travel the good road from Abergavenny; or approach by the glamorous route from Grosmont. Each way is good; each gives the warm mounting-up of excitement.

There is another road. A green road this, which I had better not recommend. If I tell you that it is a sequestered, secret narrow road, canopied for miles, ending in a buzzard's view of Skenfrith, perhaps that will deter you from seeking it.

What do you find at journey's end? Contrasting with Grosmont and Whitecastle, Skenfrith — these are the Three Towns (y Tair Tref) — sleeps in a wide green valley. Comely beyond words, the hamlet is river-blessed. Its name implies *"the river meadow of Cynfraeth,"* and I know nothing of that sixth century chieftain except that he had an eye for a site.

Skenfrith Mill, showing the castle wall and eel trap.

I walked from the mill, where Mr. Edwards preserves his famous eel-trap, along the road-side walls and then along-side the north wall to the river. At Skenfrith the Monnow makes its bow to the village, and at the weir divides to oblige the miller. The mill-race, it is clear, was originally part of the castle-moat.

Back at the entrance, where may have been a drawbridge, I recalled my earlier memories. My esteemed mentor, soldier, scholar, historian, Colonel (later Sir Joseph) Bradney had assured me that any garrison at Skenfrith must have been housed in lean-to huts of timber which had left no trace. And as I used to view that "Juliet" tower in its flat, green enclosure surrounded by strong tall curtain walls I felt inclined to agree.

Skenfrith Castle from a print dated 1732.

My smaller sketch, which is a copy of a delightful plate done in 1732, shows the Monnow and moat in the lower left-hand corner with the moat contuining under the bridge and along the north wall.

Towers stand at the four corners and a fifth mid-way along the west wall with no entrance from within. An entrance to the dungeon of the keep is surmounted by the main entrance on the first floor and roof-lines suggest that a shelter may have been built over this portal. There is no indication of a mound.

Skenfrith Castle from an "underground" room.

Skenfrith Castle, from across the weir.

Skenfrith Church.

The enterprising officials of the Ministry of Works who had already effected miracles of preservation at Tintern and Raglan doubted Sir Joseph's theory about Skenfrith. Their excavations in recent years have laid bare two ranges of rooms under the greensward, and on the western side door-ways, windows and a fireplace are in excellent preservation. These rooms are reached by thirty-two wide steps.

I asked Mr. O.E. Craster, the inspector of ancient momuments, for enlightenment. In a long informative letter, he generously disclosed information which changes completely our views about the castle. It is established now that there was a wide moat with stone-revetted walls on both the west and north sides. On the west the moat filled the whole area between the curtain-wall and the road.

Excavation has shown that there never was a castle mound at Skenfrith, but that the exciting "underground" buildings on the west side were built at the same time as the curtain-wall. This is evidenced by the fireplace which has moulded capitals to its uprights and can be dated at c.1210 — i.e. roughly as old as Magna Carta.

The causeway from the north gate to the tower was built of soil and stones from the moat. Excavations showed that the buildings on the east side of the ward, later in date, were on a higher level and it is suggested that the first buildings may have been subject to flooding.

The picturesque old tradition is that when the Normans came to Gwent the castle of Grosmont was held by Aethan of the Red Roses, White Castle by Gwyn, the blind hero, and Skenfrith by Bach, all sons of Gwaethfoed. After a period in the ownership of the Crown the castles were granted in 1201 by King John to Hubert de Burgh who was probably responsible for the structures as we know them, in part today. That they were planned as a trilateral system to prevent the wild Welsh from attacking the rich lands towards Ross is as certain as is our ignorance of any dramatic happennings throughout the ages to Skenfrith.

The Church of St. Bridget, Skenfrith.

When is Skenfrith most beautiful? In summer, autumn, winter? At twilight or by moonlight? To me it is most alluring on a May morning. The hillsides, soft in outline, veiled in silver, from the lovely church; fruit trees hold out to the pearls and opals of their blossoms; the ancient yew breathes over it a benediction; and the river sings its gay young song as it flows towards the mill.

Over the porch entrance of Skenfrith church is a primitive stone head of St. Bride but it is a poor representation of the virgin saint. Better portraits of her may be seen on the lectern within the church (where she has as accessories her lamp, green sod, oak leaves and acorns) and in the statue of her in the west wall of the tower at St. Bride's Wentloog.

A pretty waggon roof curves over the porch which, with its stone seats, niche, damaged stoup and doors, invites inspection. The inner door is a door within a door, for which an old-time blacksmith has contrived hinges which are a tribute to his skill.

Stepping through the smaller doorway we see the ancient chest on the left. On the front we read, "T.R.; I.B.; C.W.; 1661," and high above a nave arch, "R.M.; T.G.; C.W.; 1661" — expressions of joy at the new freedom gained by the accession of the Merry Monarch.

We walk along the south aisle and take two steps to examine one of the box pews which survived a Victorian "restoration." On the floor are a couple of cannon-balls, but I cannot connect them with warfare at Skenfrith.

Four hundred years old this year, John ap Philip.

A miscellany of lovely fragments of fifteenth-century glass fills the east window of the chancel. I was able to identify a bishop, roses and mitres. The famous altar, of stone similar to that used in the doorways, was replaced some years back after its maltreatment. Of about the same period is the piscina in its semi-circular niche. Corbels which supported the rood-loft remain, but there is no trace of rood or loft, screen or stairs. Behind the altar, beautifully executed carvings include the Spanish pomegranate, single (Lancaster) and Tudor roses, oak leaves and acorns of St. Bride and the fleur-de-lis.

It is, however, in the north aisle that the unique treasures of Skenfrith are housed. After many years' use as an altar-cloth the magnificent pre-Reformation cope is preserved in a glass case and forms a challenge to students of ecclesiastical symbolism. On a backcloth of velvet the vast canvas, rich with designs in silk, silver and gilt threads, is affixed; it is still possible after many centuries to trace Mary and her three angels in the centre, angels right and left. Mother and child seated, many a saint on the borders, flowers and birds in profusion, and everything suffused with a lovely impression of rose and gold.

Of equal interest is the most impressive tomb of John and Ann Morgan. "Farmer" of the three castles, M.P. for the county in 1553-4 Receiver of the Duchy of Lancaster (see the roses on the chevron), John ap Philip Morgan had married Ann Baker, also of ancient family. They had eight children; four sons are shown on one side, four daughters on the other side of the tomb, while the parents seen in my sketch are seen on the top.

Probably the tomb is 400 years old this year. Fascinating it is for men to compare John Morgan's moustache and beard with the facial decorations of Vicar Powell of Llanvetherine a century later with their own naked countenances. Engrossing it must be for women to note the bouffant sleeves — ancestors of "bishops' sleeves"? — the ruffs, the seventeen-inch waist of his sprightly wife.

Artists too, will find interest in the panels containing the portraits of the sons and daughters. Abhorring empty spaces the sculptor has included tall hats as accessories. Close at hand is the Morgan pew.

The thick walls and the draw-bolt indicate defence function in the tower. I suppose that of all the "lantern towers" from Rockfield to mid-Wales, this tower of Skenfrith is the finest. Its louvres convey the sound of its "newe six belles of 1765," while *"Ynys yr Eglwys"* and *"Ynys y Gloch,"* two river meadows were dedicated respectively to church and bell-rope maintenance.

Skenfrith

As we left it seemed that the venerable yew in the churchyard wall and the golden laburnam were bidding us a solemn and a gay godspeed.

Return along the B4521 to Norton and turn right along B4347 to reach Grosmont.

Grosmont.

Serene in its arena of hills, **Grosmont** brooks no rival among our other villages. A short street of houses, each of its own separate elevation, a glorious church, a hill-top castle overlooking an incredible river-valley, a couple of inns, two shops, and a pseudo-mediaeval town hall in the street — that is Grosmont. What then makes it unique?

Approach it from Cross Ash (on the Abergavenny-Ross road). As you complete your semi-circle around the Graig you see suddenly through the trees the spire and the castle and then houses perched, it seems, like an Italian hill-hamlet. Approach it from Llanfihangel Crucorney, along Campston hill, which we christened " Meadow-sweet Lane." Move slowly, for the glimpses of Grosmont from this height are fleeting, but of extreme beauty.

Approach it from Herefordshire over Cupid's Hill descending at about two knots. You pass a school and a few flower-filled cottage gardens and now travel-hardened though you be, gasp with delight. You pause; do you hear the sound of trumpets "on the other side?" For surely this is heaven, and you are about to enter...

When is Grosmont seen at its best? Dreamlike in December snows, idyllic in springtime when its backgound is the bluebell covered Graig *("le gros mont")*, festive in summer when its tubs and boxes and walls are gay with flowers, it is, I feel, in its most satisfying glory in autumn, when its brown roofs and spire echo the russet of its countryside.

Grosmont became crown property when Henry IV ascended the throne, and it formed the focus of Owain Glyndwr's activities. Prince Henry of Monmouth was in Hereford when he heard the news that Owain was burning Grosmont, and he sent a force to assist the garrison. In the battle that followed, Owain was routed and over eight hundred Welshmen were slain.

Grosmont Castle was a fortified residence with a hall, a circular keep, and surrounded by a deep ditch, not a water moat. It was dismantled probably in the Wars of the Roses.

Grosmont Castle.

Inside Grosmont Church.

The quaint building in the centre of the village is the Town Hall, built in 1832 on the site of a larger half-timbered hall, which had been used partly for the Justices of the Peace, and partly as a *"publick school."* There were but two offices of the ancient borough of Grosmont. One was the Mayor. The other, appointed by the Mayor, was the Ale taster, who became the next mayor.

Our visitors rave about the thrill of moonlight at Tintern. They should stand outside John Bryan's cottage at Grosmont and watch as the moon silvers the walls of the cottages, the windows light up, and the delicate spire rises like a prayer.

We begin our inspection of the village at the town hall. Built in 1832 by the Duke of Beaufort, who was lord of the manor and owner of the official market tolls, the handsome structure houses on its ground floor a fourteenth century stone of considerable interest. It is of red sandstone, about three feet high and equal width and the upper portion was once octagonal, decorated with quatrefoils.

The "market-stone" in the town hall, Grosmont.

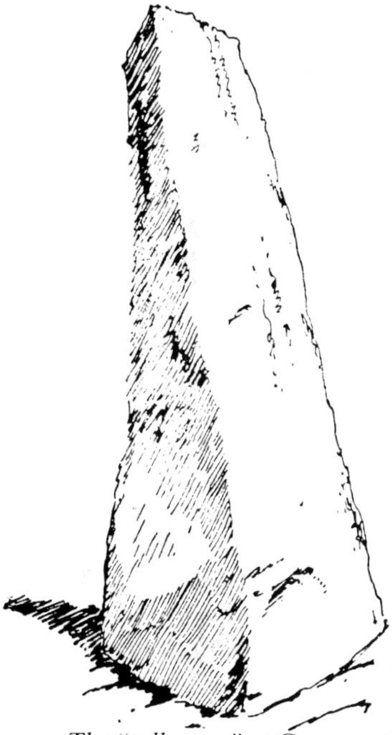

The "toll-stone" at Grosmont.

It is described by some authorities as the base of the wayside cross, but I am prepared to accept the traditional view that it was the market-stone. Market women arriving early ran to place their basket on the stone, for the first escaped toll.

Between the town-hall and the shop stands an ancient landmark still known as the toll-stone: some distance up the street stood another, long since missing. At all fairs in Grosmont the householders had the right to charge toll on merchandise placed on the land opposite their houses and between the two toll-stones.

The shop opposite the town hall has the inscription, *"1611 — H.P."* on its carved door head. Inside, the plan and ceiling beams, with their concave "stops" indicate the same age. Mrs. Nash and her mother took me around this well-preserved house. Original beams are still visible in the room behind the shop, but the show-place of the house is the room now used as a games room, where four stout beams are crossed by 19 smaller beams, reminding me of similar patterns in the western areas of our county.

In the massive fireplace beam, which is seven feet long and 18 inches deep are a recess and a peg-hole. Both were closed until eleven years ago, when the door of the small recess was opened to disclose a slipper and an old news-cutting, and at the back of the peg-hole a toothpick and human hair were found.

The lovely window-seat is matched above by a shining oaken slab, and the door to the stairs (which are baulks of oak) is controlled by a rope passing over a pulley to a weight. We were shown the garden which seemed to me to display every kind of summer flower, while the ruins of the castle stood sentinel on the hill behind.

The castle ruins are as pretty as a story-book illustration. Built within a dry-moat, outside a picturesque loop of the Monnow, the old fortress was just a fortified house with a keep and a hall 80ft. by 30ft., the ornamental chimney of which is a prominent relic.

Once there were three inns in the village — the Angel, the Duke of York and the Greyhound. The last named was the house with the big gable-front in the centre of Grosmont, and the three seem to be roughly of the same period.

As I write, the flowers on the front of the Angel are at their brilliant best. Springing from borders, tubs and window boxes they constitute a display of spectrum range from the pale hues of the clematis to the hot scarlet of the tropaoplum.

Grosmont is steeped in legend and tradition. In these degenerate days it has become part of the cult adopted by the smart sophisticated to pour ice-cold water on our old beliefs. This process lands the debunker at times in awkward spots as when a well-known writer told us that Jack O' Kent — that famous figure of the Grosmont countryside — was obviously John of Gaunt!

Similarly I find a tendency to discount the lovely legends which enrich so graciously the story of Grosmont church. Nobody has chronicled them as history, but as part of the heritage of the old town they deserve preservation.

Traditionally therefore, the church of St. Nicholas at Grosmont was built by a French architect in the service of Eleanor, queen of Henry III, and mother of Edmund, Earl of Lancaster and owner of Grosmont. It is possible that the masons who built the north transept of Hereford cathedral for Bishop Peter de Aquablanca were used by the queen for the new church at Grosmont.

Grosmont's association with the red rose goes back to the days of Aethan who occupied "Grismont," Skenfrith and White Castle before and at the time of the Norman conquest. Tenants of Aethan held their land on the payment yearly of one red rose and the Grosmont land was called *"Rosllwyn"* (rose bush). To Rosllwyn came Queen Eleanor, "the rose of Provence," and she it was who adopted the red rose as the badge of her house. Her eldest son, Henry de Grosmont had on his seal a bunch of roses, and it was his daughter who married John of Gaunt, "time-honoured Lancaster." Does it then seem ridiculous to suggest that the red rose of Lancaster may have had its origin in Grosmont?

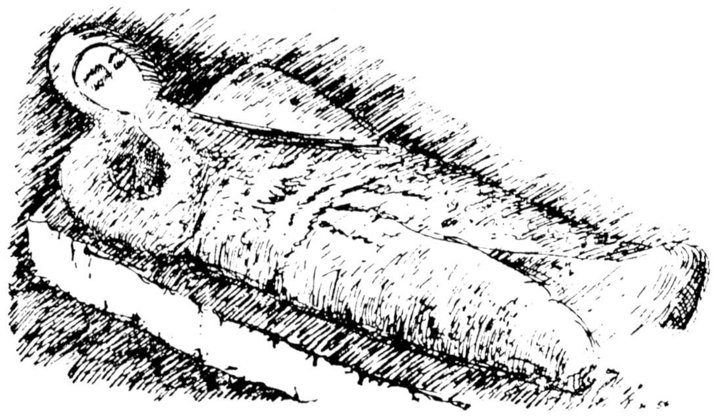

Effigy of Henry Earl of Lancaster, who died in 1361.

The church of St. Nicholas, Grosmont, from the Castle.

The splendid church of Grosmont, cruciform in plan, early English in style, with its central tower and octagonal spire, is one of the glories of Gwent. It is built of the red stone of its hill, that stone which is a rich brown in shadow, but which at a distance in late evening, glows like a rose, and I know no lovelier sight than the view of the church from the castle, when the exquisite spire rises against the background of bluebells on the Graig. There is a peal of six bells, all cast by Rudhalls of Gloucester, four in 1707, the others in 1807 and 1808.

I have always held that the Norman nave at St. Woolos and the early English nave at Grosmont are among the most impressive of any of our parish churches. The sheer bulk of the Grosmont columns seems to be emphasised by the dim lighting through the lancets by the absence of seats, and the ancient timbers above, and here I saw a wondrous vision.

At Grosmont I met Mrs. Geoghegan who had regaled me some time back with an ambrosial lunch at a hostelry named "The Hunter's Moon," which she owned at Llangattock Lingoed.

"Michael is to be married this afternoon," she announced, and then, laconically. "Come to the wedding." This adopted son of Grosmont was to marry a Llangattock lassie, and folk from both villages filled the restored portion of the church. Shafts of sunlight pierced the shadowed nave.

Of a sudden, as it seemed, a most beautiful bride appeared, followed by her little bridesmaids. Clothed in white, mystic, wonderful, they floated from sunbeam to sunbeam, and then I saw that the bride was wearing a bouquet of red roses, while her attendant maidens wore rose red ribbons in their golden hair.

Red roses in Rosllwyn! And Eleanor of Provence, Queen of England and lover of roses bent down, I am sure, to bless the bride, while Saint Nicholas patron saint of children, blessed the bridesmaids.

From Grosmont continue along the B4347 to turn left above the village and follow a minor road via Campston Hill.

I recommend to motorists — and cyclists and walkers — who use the Abergavenny-Hereford road, to forsake that series of death-traps and adopt the glorious high road over **Campston Hill**.

The Sugar Loaf from Campston hill on the Grosmont road.

For so many of us the Black Mountains are a horizon back-cloth, but from this marvellous road you have a close up view of incredible beauty. The view commands the Llanthony valley, with the conical landslide of Cwmyoy rising like an enormous Monmouth Cap. Look south to the Skirrid — our miniature Matterhorn — and its own landslide.

At the top of the road, 904 feet high, you have the richest views. On your left the country has opened out. The Hatterrall ridge slips away from its near height above Trewyn, emerald-green, past Oldcastle, past Clodock and Longtown, up towards Michaelchurch, becoming gradually more and more azure in hue until it merges into the azure of the sky.

In imagination as your eyes turn northwards, you journey through the Dore valley from Abbey Dore to Bacton (where Blanch Williams, maid of honour to Elizabeth I is buried), and Vowchurch, Turnastone, and Peterchurch; north-east along the old tram-track to St. Devereux and Hereford; east to Skenfrith and Garway — is that Ross Spire in the distance? No, brother, that is a power pylon; and south-east over our own delectable parklands around Llantilio Crosseny.

My drawing is an attempt to protray the Sugar Loaf as I saw it, silvery and mysterious, from the Campston fields, on a rare fine evening.

This Gwent of ours owes so much of her charm to her shyness. Around even her hilltop hamlets she erects a screen of trees, her gracious and ancient homesteads are rarely visible from the main roads, and the loveliest of her buildings — those little grey churches are withdrawn into the most secret haunts.

Haunts where bird-song and brook-music accompany the hymns, where the flowers of the hedgerows are culled for the decoration of font and screen, window-ledge and altar table, and where the good folk are called to worship by the same bells which called their forefathers to church when the first Elizabeth was queen.

Llangattock Lingoed — the church and inn, with the Skirrid in the background.

In a green and peaceful valley north-east of Abergavenny dreams the beautiful village of **Llangattock Lingoed**. To reach it we left the Abergavenny-Ross road just beyond Caggle Street in Llanvetherine, the narrow road edged with blue-bells leading us up and up until at a bend we drew in our breath with delighted surprise.

Ahead of us, pale blue in the silvery light, arose our Holy Mountain, the Skirrid. Below, in utter peace, framed by trees in early leaf were the church of St. Cadoc, the rectory, and the ancient inn. Every hedgerow, bush, every tree seemed full of birds, and every bird was singing, singing.

I walked to the rectory to get the key of the church. The door was opened by a happy rector's wife — or so I thought. I asked for the rector and the key, and she rippled into merry laughter. "Gracious goodness," she cried, "my husband is a retired master cotton-spinner from Wigan and we have come to Heaven some years before we are due!"

From Wigan! Every one of her many windows opened on to verdant pastoral scenery, pearled here and there by fruit-blossom. Would she ever long for factory chimneys, and clogs, for wakes, for tripe? Would she — she cut me short with an invitation to lunch, which I was sorry to turn down.

The south porch of the church, I found contained stone seats, a stoup, a studded oak door, and a pretty waggon-roof. Entering the church I recognised at once that here was a place of unique appeal, of singular and rich atmosphere, from its embattled tower, past the cowslip-encircled and very ancient font, to the chancel with its treasures all sheltering under a waggon-roof which rested on moulded beams.

Gas-lamps light the church, but the organ (with its pedal-board of one-and-a-half octaves) has its own candle-illumination and fragments of original glass remain in two of the windows.

In the chancel are preserved two of the carved box-pews which must have enriched of old the appearance of the nave. The pew on the south is dated 1634, and has interesting marks cut into the ledge; the pew opposite is inscribed E.M., referring to Edward Morgan, of Ty Mawr, in the parish of Llangattock.

In the floor of the chancel I discovered a stone, which, next to the font, may be the oldest object in the church. Cut into the stone is a T-shaped cross with no extension of the central stem, reminding me of the "Taw-crosses" of Devonshire.

Llangattock Lingoed church — the church of St. Cadoc (son of St. Gwynlliw) — stands in urgent need of repair. The parishioners are endeavouring this summer to reroof their ancient sanctuary at the cost of £1,000.

EDITOR'S NOTES

Little has changed at Llanvetherine for the Rev. David Powell is still to be seen inside the church with his splendid five-plaited beard and from the village walkers may follow a foot-path to the hilltop fortress of White Castle which is now under the protection of Cadw.

Offa's Dyke Long Distance Path now passes through the village of Llantilio Crosseny and walkers often pause at the Hostry inn to rest their feet and take refreshments. At the beautiful church of St. Teilo a musical festival is held every year in the spring attracting visitors from far and wide.

Rockfield is timeless but a few miles away the church of Llangattock-vibon-Avel has recently been restored and if you go there, seek in a corner of the churchyard the grave of Charles Rolls, for it is generally not realised that this young man who in partnership with Henry Royce gave his name to a new standard of engineering perfection, is buried here in Gwent.

At Newcastle the wistaria still adorns the Wellington Arms and in late May is a site worth seeing but sadly there is still a concrete water tank on the top of Castell Meirch!

The mill at Skenfrith is still in use and this quiet village remains unspoilt by development thankfully retaining its old world charm. The same may be said of Grosmont where the only real change from Hando's time is that the Angel is now the only pub.

Water supply in Rockfield

CHAPTER FIVE

To the Black Mountains

Llantilio Pertholey — Skirrid Fawr — Llanfihangel Crucorney — Cwmyoy — Llanthony — Capel-y-Ffin — Gospel Pass.

In Abergavenny turn opposite the Angel Hotel and follow the Hereford road through Mardy and shortly turn right to reach the hamlet of Llantilio Pertholey where the church stands near the Old Mitre Inn.

Our holy mountain, the **Skirrid,** is guarded by a ring of five ancient churches — Llanfihangel Crucorney, Llangattock Lingoed, Llanvetherine, Llanthewy Skirrid and Llantilio Pertholey. Seen from the summit, they appear as outposts to a citadel; one could imagine the five patron saints — Michael, Cadoc, James, David and Teilo — erecting a ring of prayer around their central shrine, itself dedicated to St. Michael.

St. Teilo's church, Llantilio Pertholey.

St. Teilo's church, Llantilio Pertholey, is the beautiful sanctuary which travellers see lying between road and railway a mile and a half north of Abergavenny. The Skirrid towers beyond, its landslide and ravine very clear as my sketch indicates, from the road, whence a by-road leads to the church, the "Mitre" inn, and to Maindiff Court on the Abergavenny — Ross road.

From its elegant tower to its east window St. Teilo's is full of interest. Much of that interest is human. Repairs and rebuildings have been recorded by inscriptions on stones: *"This churchyard was drain'd 1726 Mr. Geo Powell and Mr. Wm. Jones, of Crossonen churchwardens,"* on one stone. *"This wall was made and church repaired in ye year 1709"* — two *"Joneses"* churchwardens, while close at hand is a stone (on the south wall) which covers a century and a half, from Janet Dixton, 1676 to Mary Morris, who died aged 93 in 1833. The paving of the church was undertaken in 1723, when Master Powell and Jones were in charge.

St.Teilo's is equally full of architectural interest. The churchyard cross is modern (but its massive chamfered base is original) and commemorates heroes of two wars. Over the porch door is an interesting shield-shaped sundial, set askew and inside the porch the pretty waggon roof has original timbers while the holy water stoup though damaged survives.

Some of the charm of the church is due to the waggon roofs which are found throughout; even the narrow south aisle is fitted with a half-section, and the bosses and timbers as far as I could determine, have the silvery patina of great age.

The plan of this fourteenth century church is unusual. Nave arcades of three bays each lead into the aisles; the tower stands at the west end of the north aisle; the Nevill chapel on the north of the chancel, and the Wernddu chapel on the south are entered under graceful oak arches supported by stout oak columns carved with flowers and cables pattern.

A "depressed" stone arch leads into the Triley chantry, which contains a recess and an altar slab with two consecration crosses, and an atmosphere redolent of an anchorite's cell, yet even this little room has its waggon roof!

A squint pierces a stone column giving a view of the altar from the north aisle; the ancient font has three leaves carved on each chamfer of its base; two of the seventeenth century box-pews remain, each with a delightful baby's head carved on its end; and the hinges on the tower door are a craftsman's triumph.

Two questions await us. How long has a church been known on this site? The book of Llan Daf tells us that *"Lann Teiliau porth Halauc"* was given to Llandaff by Iddon, King of Gwent in the sixth century.

And what is the meaning of "Pertholey?" Pertholey — porth halauc — implies a polluted entrance.

Return to the Hereford road and turn right. At Triley Mill the A465 is joined. Follow this for about 2½ miles and then turn left for Llanfihangel Crucorney.

The Skirrid and the church, St. Michael's, Llanfihangel Crucorney.

The Skirrid from the Grosmont road.

The Holy Mountain (1596 feet high), also named **the Skirrid** ("shattered"), towers over the tiny hamlet of Llanfihangel Crucorney. A chapel of St. Michael ("Llanfihangel") stood on the summit of the Skirrid, and the mountain itself has for many centuries belonged to the manor of Llanfihangel. The Skirrid Mountain Inn, beloved of motorists and hikers, stands opposite the Court, but is not half so ancient as it imagines itself to be, for although the sign would make it of Norman date it is certainly not so old as the Court.

I remember climbing the Skirrid on Good Friday, 1953. It was a brilliant, breezy, blue day — a day for the mountains. The easy way to the Skirrid is from the Ross road. This route has many advantages in addition to its gradualness but it presents no challenge if the climber is over six and under eighty so we chose the northern approach.

Between Llwyn Frank Farm and Pen-y-Parc, we came to a snow white cottage with two snow white cats sunning themselves on the window sill.

"May we take this way to the Skirrid?" I asked the lady of the cottage. "You may," she replied, "but I don't envy you." Her voice was pretty and melodious, but under the rising intonation was a suggestion of sympathy.

We climbed the stone steps and the stile to the open field. The Skirrid towered ahead. Did I mention a challenge? Matterhorn memories — for I had seen the Matterhorn at a distance — seemed perhaps an over-statement of the job ahead of us: the gradient of the eastern slope appeared to be only slightly less than the precipice on the right.

After some exploration we found the winding "pony path". My companion, intolerant of my speed, went ahead at what seemed a supersonic velocity and was soon out of sight, while I enjoyed the rhythm of a few steps and a view, a few steps and a view.

A shout from above announced that one of us had reached the summit. I toiled upwards. The hours passed. Then with a gasp of relief, I flung myself into Jack o' Kent's heel-print — for you should know that the hollow in the top of the Skirrid which marks the site of the Llanfihangel (St. Michael's Church) was formed when Jack o' Kent leaped the four miles from the summit of the Sugar Loaf. Not satisfied with this and egged on by the contemptuous sniff of the Devil, Jack thereupon threw three enormous stones over twelve miles to Trellech, where they remain.

Among the secret places in which the Catholics of North Monmouthshire met during their times of persecution ones of the most easily observed must have been the summit of the Skirrid. It was visible from Llanfihangel Crucorney, the home of Squire Arnold and the name of Arnold was the one most dreaded by the Catholics. Yet the legend of those meetings persisted and, through-out later centuries, anniversary services were held on the mountain-top on the eve of Michaelmas.

When Archdeacon Coxe climbed the Skirrid in 1800, he could see Hereford Cathedral. It has been one of my ambitions to see the Cathedral from the Skirrid and on this clear afternoon I had great hopes.

Coxe wrote, tout court: "*The fpires of Hereford Cathedral gleam in the diftant profpect,*" and he had not the benefit of my prismatic binoculars. But no cathedral spires or towers gleamed for us.

Yet the views south over the familiar landmarks and the Channel, East where White Castle and all the little villages were crystal clear, North, where the Hereford hills threw their shadows on the Golden Valley, and West — ah! never have I seen the Black Mountains in such minute detail, with Pen-y-Fal and his big brothers in calm majesty and Cwmyoy like a giant carbuncle — such prospects dispelled my disappointment at missing the Hereford spires.

After noting with satisfaction that the National Trust had taken over the mountain, we scrambled down through the heather while my companion gleefully experimented with his new double boomerang.

And if you know a more appetising idea, after climbing the Skirrid, than toasted and buttered hot cross buns and tea, do write and tell me.

In the village of **Llanfihangel Crucorney** is another church of St. Michael — this one on a lower eminence — and so I am able to include in my sketch two churches dedicated to the same saint. That one of the churches is invisible is of no import.

So much for 'Llanfihangel,' but what of 'Crucorney'? Bradney explains it as Crug (rock or hill), but we should not overlook the fact that in 1291 the parish was named Sci Michio Kilcornli, which would imply that it was the cell of a saint.

The church consists of tower, nave, chancel and porch, and was rebuilt during the last century. In the porch the old roof timbers and bosses (fleur-de-lis) and (Tudor rose) have been retained, and affixed to the porch wall is the tombstone, dated 1766, of James Hughes, the village blacksmith, with the epitaph:

My Sledge and hammer lies reclin'd,
My bellows, too, have lost his wind,
My Fires extinct, my Forge Decay'd,
And in ye Dust, my Vice is laid,
My Coal is Spent, my Iron is Gone,
My Nails are Drove, my Work is Done.

Near the porch stands the beautiful wrought font. A memorial stone which formed part of the floor now leans against the south wall near the font.

High in the west wall of the nave is the window which enabled the bellringers to see the progress of the service in the chancel. The battlemented tower is a well known landmark from every direction; on its east wall can be seen the evidence that the original roof of the nave was higher in pitch than the present roof. I found it of interest that the bosses in the chancel roof (which include the sacred monogram, fleur-de-lis enhanced with acorns, etc., Tudor Rose, a masonic device, and a fascinating design incorporating a floriated cross and two birds) are repeated in the floor tiles.

The silver chalice of the church bears the arms of John Arnold, M.P. for Monmouth, resident of Llanfihangel Court, and claiming descent from Ynyr, King of Gwent. It is inscribed:

16 St. Michalis Crucorny 74
Ex Dono Johani Arnold

It is to the paternal arms of the Arnolds that the fleur-de-lis in the porch and chancel refer.

It seems that the original inn at Llanfihangel Crucorney was the house now known as Millbrook, opposite the mill on the old road. The famous hostelry which we know as the **Skirrid Mountain Inn** was then perhaps a hostelry, but certainly a court of justice.

The Skirrid mountain inn, Llanfihangel Crucorney.

Records (which I have not yet examined) survive which tell of two brothers, John and James Crowther, tried at the court house, John for stealing sheep, for which he was hanged, and James, who was gaoled for nine months for robbery with violence on the Grosmont road.

That trial is reputed to have taken place in 1110. Somewhere in the inn, covered by plaster, is an inscription, "J.H.T. 1306" — so I was told — but whether the date is in Roman or Arabic is not remembered. The date on the board outside the inn-1100 A.D. — is conjectural, and probably suggested by the date of the Crowther trial, although I note that the "Skirrid Mountain" inn is named in a recent publication as the second oldest inn in the British Isles.

It would be pleasant, after a careful examination of the structure to be able to confirm its great age. Strict veracity compels me to record that, though a more ancient house may have stood on the site, no relic survives which would date the present building before late Elizabethan days — c. 1600.

Standing on the cobbled "pull-in," I could imagine with ease what this — the rear — facade looked like before its re-construction. Six relieving arches, three on each side of the oaken doorway, show where the original windows appeared. These lighted one big room, running the length of the house, and warmed by a splendid fireplace.

Alongside this fireplace, to the right, hidden now behind the bar, is the tiny "grog-grate," where the poker was heated for mulling the ale. Above the fireplace is the little shelf where the "devil's brew" — a pot of ale for his satanic majesty — was reserved.

Now this "devil's brew" has always seemed to me to be a variant of the practice, common in many of the old houses of Gwent, of leaving a jug of milk for "Pwcca" on the doorstep at night, thus appeasing the mischievous sprite who might otherwise indulge in many a nocturnal prank.

And not far away of course is Allt-yr-Ynys, one of the places where Shakespeare was told of Y Pwcca who became the "Puck" of his "Midsummer Night's Dream"!

My old friends Mr. and Mrs. Barbour showed me, not for the first time around their fascinating house. We examined the ceiling beams with their concave "stops," the panelling in the dining room, "originally in a ship," my host assured me; we admired the stout masonry in the cellar, where a curved stone structure supported the great fireplace above; and I listened once again to the story of the shaft which ran from the cellar underneath the road.

We stood at the foot of the fine oak staircase where delicacy and refinement are wedded to strength and dignity. It was no mean craftsman who could contrast the bulk of the posts and pendants with the grace of the intermediate members.

Climbing the oak treads we arrived first at the "mesne" floor where Mr. Barbour showed me into the "cell," where the prisoners were incarcerated. Holes pierced into the door frame enabled the jailer to keep his wards under surveillance.

On the first floor we entered the courtroom — now the sittingroom — and the adjoining Judge's bedroom. The banqueting hall is now a lounge and bedroom, and here the weight of the oak baulks above the windows is taken by posts.

"Between the ceiling and the floor," said Mr. Barbour, "we found the space filled with barley-husks." My readers may remember that a similar space in Trellech Grange was filled with hazel nuts.

In all the timber of the inn the only trace of decay is in the uppermost flight of the stairs. The repair is in the hands of a craftsman who, like his predecessors, guarantees his work to last, not for years, but for centuries, and as if to inspire him, an original window with oak mullions, high in the gable, looks down as he works. It is as sound as when it was installed.

From the west windows the views over the Honddu are of mountains and valley clefts, with white homesteads warm and cosy down below, and others clinging to the upland slopes, amidst the green goodness which is Gwent.

During the Ice Age, nearly half a million years or less ago, mid-Wales lay under a vast sheet of ice. Glaciations from this ice shaped the valleys in our own Black Mountains; one glacier dictated the course of the Honddu ("black water") in the Llanthony Valley.

Thousands of tons of detritus rocks, stones, rubbish were deposited at the mouth of the valley as a quandrant-shaped moraine. This in turn dictated the later course of the Honddu, for while the Grwyne streams flowed westward into the Usk, the Honddu swung north-east-ward to join the Monnow.

When we drive down the Llanthony valley we see ahead of us a long green embankment cut through on the right of the railway. That is the glacial moraine. On the moraine are built the church of St. Michael, the Skirrid Mountain Inn, the vicarage, a garage and **Treturret.**

Treturret, Llanvihangel Crucorney.

When in 1958, I organised a survey of our Black Mountains, my guide was Mr. Herbert Atkins of Treturret, whom I christened Herbert Mihangel because his handsome house was in Llanfihangel.

The many happy hours spent in company with Herbert and Gwladys Mihangel, sometime on the ridges and summits, sometimes in the sequestered glens, gave me an intimate knowledge of the region and its people — which I could not have acquired alone.

"It would be exciting to have lunch on a glacial moraine," we felt when the invitation came to lunch at Treturret. So through Gwent in the time of daffodils we drove northward, took the Hereford road out of Abergavenny, crawled through Llanfihangel Crucorney to the car park, waited for a lull in the traffic, and shot across to Treturret, where in the warmth of a typical Mihangel welcome, Ysiad and I forgot glaciers and moraines.

And what a site for a house! From all the east windows of tower and house, bright in the noon sunshine, the view commanded a comely green valley from which arose hills topped by the Grosmont road, and in the south the Matterhorn (in miniature) of the Skirrid. That incredible peak seemed distant, perhaps half a mile; it is nearer a mile and a half. I recalled how the Bennet boys used to ride on their ponies from the Court to the summit and back before breakfast.

In borders around the lawn and from a dozen stone troughs, daffodils and tulips sang to the sun. Birds joined in the midday chorus. We turned to examine the house, and all its walls and battlements built of our own old red sand-stone. Treturret seemed, like all the houses and churches of the region to have grown out of the ground.

"It was probably a 'ty'r agent' — an agent's house," said Herbert, "and was later extended. The heavy stone roof is held up by grand oaken timbers; roof, timbers, and walls combined to form a building made for posterity. I suspect that the domestic architecture of today may not last like Treturret."

In 1799 Archdeacon Coxe climbed the Skirrid and suffered an attack of giddiness at the summit. After descending the mountain he walked around to the groves of oaks and Spanish chestnuts which formed the avenue leading to **Llanfihangel Court** which (possibly a reaction after his giddiness) he dismissed thus:

The White Lady of Llanvihangel.

"It is now inhabited by a farmer, and contains nothing but some old furniture a few family pictures, and some good impressions of Hogarth's prints.

He does however include a charming little illustration of the house by Sir Richard Hoare showing it much as it is today, except for the outbuildings on the left which have disappeared. The Skirrid and its landslide are shown to the left, and by a remarkable coincidence a 'white lady' is seen descending the steps.

Seen from the north front, the Court is a solid structure, with two gables at each end and a charming dormer window over the central entrance. Picturesque in truth is the formal courtyard at the south-east where above the flagged floor and lily pond arise the grey walls with handsome windows, surmounted by walnut-hued roofs and tall stone chimneys — two of them 'clustered' Elizabethan. Steps lead up from the courtyard to the outhouses and the stables, where I took the chance of sketching the famous oak columns, traditionally from a wrecked Armada galleon and erected here by Spanish prisoners.

The courtyard Llanfihangel Court.

Away beyond, stretch the remains of the chestnut avenue — magnificent trees, rising like fluted stone columns, almost as old as the house. In the chestnut avenue is a deep well to which is attached a memory. Long ago the beloved and only son of the house drank from a pewter cup, was poisoned and died. Frantic with grief, the father collected all his pewter, which was never seen again.

Within the court, all is well-proportioned and beautiful. Colonel Hopkinson and his lady have furnished their home with their own treasures, and as we walked around the rooms the family portraits seemed to greet us. One Court beauty vied with another, but for sheer loveliness I should choose the superbly painted Lady Congleton, arrayed as maid of honour to Queen Victoria.

The priceless seventeenth-century rose ceiling displayed not only Tudor roses and oak leaves, but also the queerly decorated fleur-de-lis like those I had noted in the village church. Doubtless the Arnolds had the right — from Ynyr, king of Gwent — to use the fleur-de-lis, but by what dispensation could they cause acorns — if they are acorns! — to spring between the petals?

Llanvihangel Court

After my inspection of so many Monmouthshire houses it was pleasant to place Llanfihangel Court "in period." The earliest portion of 1559 is the east wing and the remainder is of the early seventeenth century.

Of the many splendid rooms I must note the "White Room" where once was seen "a little man with green eyes" and the "King's Room" where Charles I slept. The head of the bed on which he slept is preserved and bears the inscription...... "KOFIA DY DDECHRE" (Remember thine origin).

I was glad to see again the fine coat-of-arms of Charles I painted on wood and decorated with mother of pearl, which young Mr. Bennet had discovered reversed behind a wall panel.

One of the most characteristic rooms is "Queen Elizabeth's Room", in which an imposing four poster bed with an ornate canopy may have rested the much travelled queen. Of the dramatis personae I need but record that the manor was held in the days of Henry VI by Thomas ap John ap Gwilym Jenkin of Wernddu, that a descendant Rhys Morgan built the east wing and that by way of the Earl of Worcester the Court was sold to the Arnolds.

It was John Arnold of Llanfihangel, who made himself famous — and infamous — by his fanatical persecution of the Roman Catholics who dared to celebrate Mass in the little Llanfihangel chapel on the Skirrid summit. An interesting comment is Coxe's note, written a century later:

"To this place many Roman Catholics
in the vicinity are said to repair

annually on Michaelmas eve
and perform their devotions, The earth of
this spot is likewise considered
as sacred and was formerly carried away
to cure diseases, and to sprinkle on
the coffins of those who were interred."

Turn left at the Skirrid Mountain Inn and bear left at the bottom of the hill by Bridge Cottage to follow the scenic route through the Vale of Ewyas, past Cwmyoy and on to Llanthony, Capel-y-Ffin the Gospel Pass and perhaps down the other side of the Black Mountains to reach Hay-on-Wye.

Bridge Cottage, Llanfihangel Crucorney.

Seen from the road, **Bridge Cottage** has changed little during three centuries. Slates replace the old stone tiles, the chimneys are now of bricks, and the walls have been "rendered." Yet the chimney-ledges, the deep-set ground floor windows, the bar-dripstones, the doorway and the general air of demure assurance demands that we shall cherish it. I suspect that the building of the old bridge at the ford over the Honddu accounted for the siting of the cottage. This would be an appropriate origin for the home of a bridge builder and roadmaker.

The Vale of Ewyas

Soon after turning into the Llanthony valley you will descry amid the heights ahead a weird bulbous summit. That is the Cwmyoy landslide, a mighty fragment torn away from the Hatterrall ridge. Seen from the front, part of the hilltop is shaped like a yoke, accounting for the name "Cwmyoy" — the valley of the yoke; seen from afar, the landslide itself seems like an immense boil on the shoulder of the Hatterrall.

If you are among the fortunate few who use their legs, you must have the magnificent approach via the Hatterrall ridge. Leave the bus at Pandy, take the Longtown road and climb the lane past Trewyn house to the ridge, along which you will have noble views of Herefordshire, of the mountain system, of the blue bells, of the landslide, and, if you wish, a delightful descent past the ruins of Walter Savage Landor's house to Llanthony Abbey.

The motorist will turn right at the Queen's Head inn, and thread the narrow lane down and up into the village, parking at the foot of the rise to the church. The first view of the church justifies your journey, for the little brown sanctuary wobbles — yes, wobbles — on a slope above which towers the landslide. "Wobbles"? Well, the tower bends perilously towards the hillside, while the chancel threatens at any moment to disintegrate into the valley. I know little about Martin, the saint of the church, but he has had a potent influence in stabilising a church which might have evolved in the creative mind of Walt Disney.

Cwmyoy Church

We saw **Cwmyoy church** during the harvest festival of 1953. Every available window-sill, niche and shelf and corner was decorated with flowers and fruit, and to our intense delight on every pew-end was affixed a Cwmyoy corn-dolly, made by loving hands at Blaenyoy. Since then we have seen many ornate species, but we retain our affection for the simple hoop-dolly of Cwmyoy.

A relic of fertility-worship, the corn-dolly has been a pagan symbol of the last sheaf in the reaping field for thousands of years. In its varying forms it is known throughout this island and southern Europe.

The chancel of Cwmyoy church is a remarkable example of a "weeping-chancel". In many of our churches the axis of the chancel slews sideways, and it seems that the builders planned it thus, for if the slant had been due to the landslide it should have followed the slant of the tower.

Deep in the soil behind a derelict cider mill a "crucifixion-stone," was discovered. My friend the late vicar suggested to me that this stone once rested on the pedestal which is still to be seen in the vicarage garden.

There is an undoubted track — possibly a pilgrims' way to the abbey — which passes this pedestal, in which case the sculpture may have been part of a wayside Calvary such as we find in France.

I have taken many visitors to Cwmyoy. All experienced the wonderful exhilaration of the holy upland place. There is little change in Cwmyoy since 1682, when Tom Price was buried there. See his memorial:

"Thomas Price he takes his
nap
In our common mother lap
Waiting to heare the Bride-
groom say
Awake my dear and come
away"

The leaning church at Cwmyoy.

The Vale of Ewyas.

Llanthony Priory

On a halcyon June afternoon Ysiad and I threaded our way through the enchanted Vale of Ewyas, where a vastly improved road took us towards Llanddewi Nant Honddu, the church of St. David on the brook of the black water — in short, Llanthony.

Improved the road is in our time. How did Archdeacon Coxe react to the track in 1800?

"In this road, which with more propriety could be termed a ditch, we heard the roar of the torrent beneath, but seldom enjoyed a view of the circumjacent scenery... I would not recommend timid persons to pass this way in a carriage, for in the whole course of my travels I seldom met with one more inconvenient and unsafe. Excepting in very few places, there is not room for a single horse to pass by a chaise; and should two carriages meet neither could proceed until one was drawn back to a considerable distance. The soil is boggy in wet and rough in dry weather; the ruts worn by the small Welsh cars are extremely deep, and often times we were prevented from being overturned only by the narrowness of the road and the steepness of the sides."

In silence we glided around bend after bend, until almost with a sigh, we reached the sleeping hamlet of **Llanthony.**

Llanthony Hamlet. The post office school house and disused mill.

Mr. Powell, who has spent his long life at the post office on the left, indicated the school house in the centre and the mill on the right, long silent, though we could trace the mill race.

"Mill in the Llanthony valley" was a favourite subject with our old painters in watercolour. In water colour too, J.M.W. Turner rendered his superb vision of "Llanthony Priory, Monmouthshire" — a picture sold in 1960 for £5,000. Where would these travelling artists put up at Llanthony?

On a map of 1880 the hamlet includes a corn mill, a saw mill, a smithy, a school for boys adjoining St. David's church and two inns, the Traveller's Rest and the Half Moon. The main track up the valley must have been joined near the hamlet by the ancient way — pack-horse track and pilgrims' way — which had traversed the opposite bank.

Both the inns stood on this track, but the Travellers' Rest is only a memory.

At the foot of the hill the cluser of brown cottages caught my fancy. Set against the swelling green of Bal Mawr they were a study in old-time grace and harmony. At the **Half Moon Inn,** Mr. and Mrs. Stockwell greeted me: "Of course we have one of your uncle's clocks. It is so accurate that we never alter it.

Imagine my thrill when I saw the wall clock with his name, "John Hando, Brecon," on the face. Jeweller of Brecon, he kept all the church clocks of the county in order, and one of the great joys of our holidays in Brecon was to accompany him in his pony-drawn governess car from church to church.

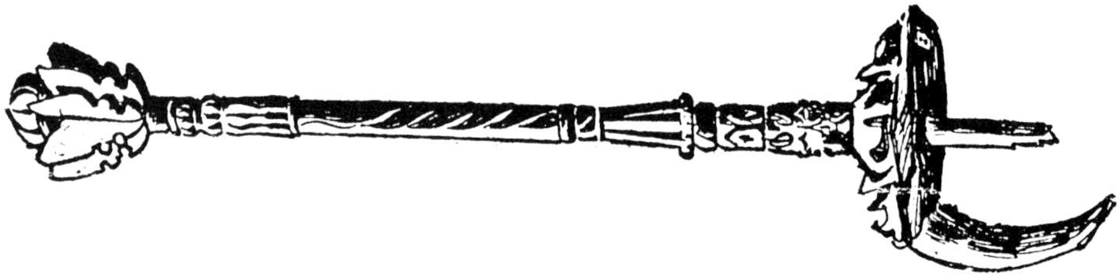

Ceremonial iron mace found at Half Moon Inn, llanthony.

Hanging on the same wall as the clock was the strange iron object shown in my sketch. It was discovered recently amidst miscellaneous lumber in an unused room of the inn. Obviously it is a cutlass-handled ceremonial mace, but its age and specific purpose and its location at the Half Moon, are conjectural. One could with ease picture an old-time thief bartering the mace for old-time cwrw-da...

Turning up the Abbey lane. I parked the car where David found solitude and peace in his humble cell some 1,300 years ago. He is recalled of course by the little **church of St. David's,** dwarfed by the majestic abbey, half as old.

St. David's Church, Llanthony.

Tradition avers that St. David set up his cell fourteen centuries ago on the site of the chancel of this little church. This was "the humble chapel, decorated only with moss and ivy" referred to by Giraldus Cambrensis (who did not visit the site) and by several other ancient chroniclers.

Five centuries later William de Lacy, weary after a day's hunting of deer, rested alongside the ruins of the cell. The effect of fatigue and the utter serenity of this sequested shrine was immediate. Listen to one of the monks......

"He laid aside his belt and girdled himself with a rope; instead of fine linen, he covered himself with hair cloth; and instead of his soldiers's robe he loaded himself with heavy irons. The suit of armour he still wore as a garment to harden himself against the temptations of his old enemy, Satan... He thus crucified himself and continued this hard armour on his body until it was worn out with rust and age."
(Dugdale's Monastikon).

Llanthony Priory.

The fame of William the hermit reached the court of Henry I and soon he was joined by Ernesi, chaplain to Queen Maud. It is safe to allot the chancel of St. David's to the efforts of the two anchorites in 1108 A.D.

That "chancel" of today was the whole church of 1108. As I stood facing the altar an "abstract" of moss and ivy, ropes and hair-cloth and rusty armour formed in imagination the background to the images of the three saints — so frail, so threadbare, so pale and famished, yet shining in their holy solitariness — who had lived on this little plot of ground. And it was that tiny sanctuary which decided the siting of the vast Llanthony Abbey.

The "nave" of St. David's demands careful study. Where else have we four doorways, two fireplaces (one on each of two floors), a sewer running across the west end, and signs of window-seats under two of the south windows? This was without doubt the infirmary hall — "hospitium" — of the monks, joined to their infirmary church.

I walked around the church noting the Early Norman windows, the one square-headed Tudor replacement, the door-ways. In the barn, opposite the western door-way in the south wall of the church is a further ancient doorway which needs explanation.

A stroll between the outhouses into the field south-east of the abbey ended with a shock as I gazed into a pit, some fifteen feet wide, part filled with rubbish of all kinds. It was still possible, however, to see some of the dressed stones and L-shaped nest-holes of the **Llanthony dovecote,** unique in our island.

The ruined underground dovecote, Llanthony.

Discovered by workmen sixty years ago, this was our only underground dovecote, with its ground-floor, and entrance between wing-walls, seven feet below surface. Above the circular walls with their nest-holes, the roof was built bee-hive fashion with a capstone 4ft. 4in. in diameter in which was a central hole of 1ft. 4in. diameter. The walls were four feet thick, and an observer in 1905 suggested that the columbarium was built so at times it might be covered with earth.

My duty is clear. If the good farmer agrees, this unique relic must be cleared of rubbish, among which fragments of the roof and capstone will be found. Rovers and scouts, hikers and pony-trekkers from Capel-y-Ffin — here is a project worthy of your zest!

A century back, in September, 1864, died Walter Savage Landor, friend of Southey and Robert Browning of all people! How those two must have wrangled! — This strange and turbulent genius seemed doomed to arouse antipathy.

Expelled from Rugby, sent down from Oxford, he sought in 1809 at the age of 34, to realise himself in a new environment. He realised himself! In the incredibly green Llanthony this ex-soldier who had fought in Spain against Napoleon, lived in the Prior's house adjoining the abbey and planned a vast scheme.

I have told readers previously how Landor spent thousands of pounds planting cedar saplings, building bridges and a house, importing cattle and at the same time alienating the people of the valley.

After a century what remains? A trace of house-foundations opposite the abbey, an exquisite single-arched bridge at Henllan, a few timber bridges, and, best of all, that nostalgic cry from Italy:

Llanthony!......
I loved thee by the streams of yore
By distant streams I love thee more.

That he entertained other men of letters — including Southey — at Llanthony is certain. That he wrote some of his lesser known works in the Prior's house is probable. Yet in three years his wildly impractible schemes and prodigal expenditure brought the inevitable end.

Landor's mother took over the estate and made him an allowance and he saw Llanthony no more.

Capel-y-Ffin beyond Llanthony.

A little white chapel it is. Towering above it to the north-west is the magnificent green dome of Daren Llwyd, itself a "Knob," just as its prolongation leads on to the better-known Lord Hereford's Knob — "Y Tumpa." On the right is the superb ridge which culminates in Hay Bluff, twin to "Y Tumpa."

From the southern slopes of Lord Hereford's Knob a nant y Mynydd (mountain stream) cascades down to meet another — the infant Honddu, which has carved its romantic way down from Hay Bluff. The two streams meet at **Capel-y-Ffin,** half a carved mile into Breconshire from Monmouthshire.

I met the vicar, who ministers also to the good folk of Llanigon beyond Hay Bluff. Full of joy he was because, although he has a membership of six, on that afternoon his congregation numbered 14. We examined the porch inscription —

L.P.W.
I.I.M.
1817

We pondered over a small stone column which may have been part of the churchyard cross; we wondered why the eight ancient yews were planted in a semi-circle; we agreed that the circular churchyard edging a track-cum-packtrail told of immense age, and then, after the vicar had left for Llanigon, I spent an engrossing half-hour among the tomb-stones. From my notes I append two gems.

The first was *"In memory of Noah, ye son of Noah Watkins, who died aged 8 years in 1738. This child said he would not take A hundred pounds in money for Breaking the sabbath, but keep it holy."* That is cut in the flowing script which we associate with the *"Beggars' Opera."*

I vouch also for the second which records the death in 1843 of Tom Jones —

"Aged 1 Years and 101 months.
When the Archangel's trump
shall sound,
And souls to bodies join,
Millions will wish their lives
below
Had been as short as mine."
"Aged 1 years and 101 months"!

The monumental mason's "sould" was above such sordid matters as numeration. Unable to convert "eleven" into figures he combined 10 and 1 into 101 Thus Tom Jones aged 1 year and 11 months.

Roaming amid these quaint relics, I was suddenly halted by the lettering on two modern stones. Such perfection of shape and spacing proclaimed that Eric Gill had cut the inscriptions, and I was not surprised to hear from Mrs. Gwynne Rees of Clomendy, that our great sculptor, while at Capel-y-Ffin monastery, had employed Charlie Stones as his handyman, and on his death had cut the inscription, which I have copied.

Back on the packhorse road, I took a last look at the white chapel. How did Kilvert describe it in his diary? *"Short, stout and boxy, with its little bell turret, the whole building reminding me of an owl"* — and the two window-eyes and porch-beak fit that perfectly, while the owl has but one ear — the bell turret. That bell turret was the primitive prototype of the timber turrets at Skenfrith and elsewhere, and the louvre arrangement of the upper timbers at Capel-y-Ffin, like the more elaborate constructions of the later turrets, allows the sound of the bells to escape, at the same time protecting the bells.

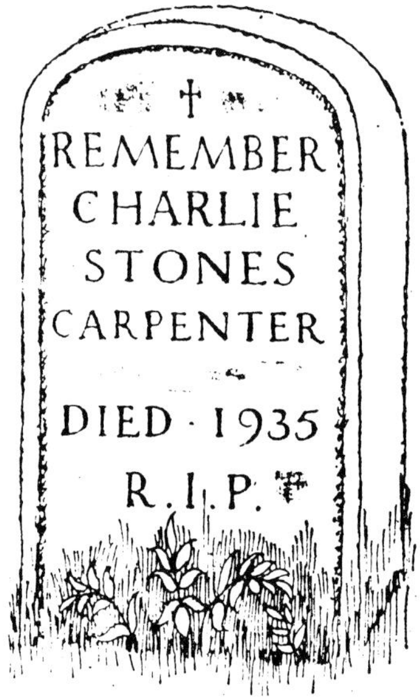

Lettering by Eric Gill in Capel-y-Ffin churchyard.

The Baptist chapel at Capel-y-Ffin.

Like the Anglican chapel, the **Baptist chapel** over the river at Capel-y-Ffin is whitewashed. A chimney, half in and half out of the building runs up from the fireplace in the east wall. Great yews as old as the chapel tower over the many tombstones. Some of the tombstone inscriptions are in Welsh; one, in English, is surmounted by a charming profile cut in the stone of Susanna, wife of James Watkins, of Sychfra, Cwmyoy.

"This lovely rose, so young and fair,
Was called by early doom,
Just to show how sweet a flower
In Paradise would bloom".

On the south wall of the chapel a stone is inscribed — *"Messrs. William and David Prosser Brought the Ministry of the Gospel to their House in the Year 1757. And secured this Place for that sacred use for the time being."*

It would be an absorbing task, had one the time, to trace the growth of the Baptist cause in these remote regions, and to relate the little white house of God at Capel-y-Ffin with similar conventicles at Olchon, Llanwenarth and Abergavenny.

Inside the chapel, three steps on each side lead to the pulpit. Candlesticks on each side of the bible, the harmonium below, pews for the deacons and the congregation, the gallery on the north and east, lighting now by inverted gas mantles, and the air of reverent simplicity, conjure up in my mind the 200 years of worship in this "Babell." For fifty of those years the Rev. Morgan Lewis laboured here and he died in his ninetieth year.

Some writers find "contemptible" the architecture of our little Welsh temples. By some grace implanted in me when young I can move from the massive grandeur of Llanthony Abbey to the two tiny white chapels at Capel-y-Ffin with no senses of anticlimax.

The monastery of Father Ignatius at Capel-y-Ffin.

As I walked up the narrow stony lane, its hedgerows bright with pink wild-roses, I saw in my imagination a saintly face with burning eyes, a frail figure garbed in Benedictine habit, knotted scourge girdle, a silver cross on his breast and a golden cross hanging from a rosary of black beads. This was the man who dared in a Scots episcopal church to preach the eucharistic presence, and the veneration of God's Virgin Mother, the man who had aroused fierce hatred in English hearts, yet had faced the mobs of London's dockland. And in conflict with Charles Bradlaugh, had won to his side an audience of atheists by the sheer magic of his personality.

Robbed by a trick of his monastery and property at Norwich, Father Ignatius came to the Llanthony valley in 1869 hoping to house a neo-Benedictine brotherhood in the abbey. When the owner objected, he bought 33 acres and the right of a sheep-walk above Capel-y-Ffin, laid a foundation stone and administered the first mass at an improvised altar in the old farm-house of Ty-Gwyn.

By the July he had installed his small community in a shed. The story of their transport, of their hardships during that first winter (when their only physical comfort was an open fire on the damp earth floor of the refectory) of the super-human efforts to cut the stones, bring them on rough tracks to the site, and raise them to considerable heights, is a minor saga.

Frequently the monk of Llanthony left for the great cities where he preached and collected so much money that in spite of the enormous expense — the reredos from Munich cost £2,000 — he was able to aver that no stone entered the precincts until the money was available for its payment.

What remains from those extraordinary days? I met Miss Joyce Newport who, with Mrs. Eric Gill owns the property which is now a unique guest house. She gave me *carte blanche* to investigate, and this is what I saw.

The church, open to the sky, is an awful ruin. In the floor, smashed by a fallen heavy corbel is the cross which marks the grave of Father Ignatius, "PRIMUSOVE ABBAS, R.I.P. OBIIT 16 OCT. MCMVIII." Gone is all the splendour; the church, chancel only, was never completed; of the altar, stalls, canopies, nuns' galleries, reredos, great organ, nought remains; the walls are in such a parlous state that visitors enter the ruins at their own risk.

The monastery buildings, on the other hand, far from being as a recent writer described them, "in ruins," are in excellent preservation. They form a block around the garth, the lower story being the "cloister" which is not a cloister. Nearly all the windows are pointed and instead of opening on to the magnificent hills, give views of the garth.

The superior's cell, shown in my drawing under the oriel window in the centre, the refectory, sacristy, common room, guests' dining room and sitting-room (once the "prophets' chamber") and cubicles and library retain the authentic monastic atmosphere, and on the sunny afternoon of my visit surprised me (for I have no element of the anchorite) by their attractiveness.

Eric Gill whose portrait and message greet the visitor at the entrance, had founded, with Hilary Peppler and Desmond Chute, the Ditchling Guild. Dedicated to beauty, goodness and truth, this company of craftsmen had as their motto, "Man's work should bear witness to his love of God," and became members of the Third Order of St. Dominic.

The publicity which the guild attracted was anathema to Gill. In a famous exodus he and three families — thirteen people, a pony, chickens, cats, dogs, goats, geese, ducks, magpies and luggage — hired a lorry at Pandy and arrived at Capel-y-Ffin in a typical Welsh cloudburst, to find that their new home had no conveniences except water.

With immense energy they faced their jobs, and soon became a self-contained community, the others running the house and farm while Gill cut tombstone inscriptions and wood-engravings, especially for the Golden Cockerel Press.

It was at Capel-y-Ffin that he devised his world famous alphabet of sans-serif type, and others, for the Monotype Corporation. With his engravings and sculptures and lettering, mass before breakfast and frequent psalms and prayers in the chapel which he built (and which still survives), Eric Gill strove after the Dominican way of life, "My dearest thoughts," he wrote, "and all my desiring shall be always in His presence."

With his people he took long walks in the enchanted land around the monastery. "One of the loveliest things in the world is the walk from Rhiw Wen at the top of the valley back to Capel-y-Ffin," he used to say, and who would challenge him?

He was at the monastery from 1924 to 1928, when he chartered two railway trucks and three pantechnicons for another exodus, but in 1930 he bought the monastery for his eldest daughter, who lived there until 1956.

From Capel-y-Ffin we continued to climb pas the last green coppice, up and up, past the new youth hostel at Castle farm, and parted company with the young Honddu at 1,300 ft. altitude.

Within two miles we topped the pass at the breathtaking "Bwlch yr Efengyl" — **the gospel pass** —a name which is variously explained. Some authorities say that it dates back to the day when Archbishop Baldwin came this way, others that the Lollards came singing along this way, and still others that when the Baptists were turned out of their chapels, they came this way to another.

For us, as always, there was one programme. We parked the car on the Bwlch, and while Ysiad enjoyed her mountaineering vicariously the two boys and I set off for the summit.

The car stood at an altitude of 1,775 ft., between two splendid heights — Hay Bluff, on the right, reaching 2,219 ft., and Lord Hereford's Knob ("The Tumpa" on your map) 2,263 ft.

Here let me dispel any nervous doubts. This is the easiest of climbs. From the pass the rise on the right is steep and covered with loose scree: that way, of course was followed by the two boys; I took the green rise to the left and came by a gentle right-hand curve to the summit; the three of us added stones to the cairn at the top.

And the view? — On two visits we have seen over the heavenly mid-distance the mountains of central Wales, and beyond, like still clouds, Cader Idris and Plinlimmon. My friend Herbert Mihangel has seen in perfect conditions, these two mountains, and, to the right, Snowdon, ninety miles away!

EDITOR'S NOTES

In Llanfihangel Crucorney the church nave has for some years been without a roof. Egon Ronay has visited the Skirrid Mountain Inn and given his sign of approval.

Skirrid Fawr is now a popular ascent from a car park on the Ross road (B4521) where a stile and footpath sign indicate the way. The path leads into a wood where steps have been built by the National Park Service to reduce erosion and make the climb easier. On gaining the ridge it is an exhilarating walk with impressive views all round and near the summit the site of St. Michael's chapel can be seen. Skirrid Fawr like its shapely neighbour — the Sugar Loaf is now owned by the National Trust.

Returning to Llanfihangel Crucorney, Treturret is of course a private house but visitors are allowed to enter Llanfihangel Court on weekends and Bank Holidays during the summer.

Bridge Cottage has been extended and altered but at Cwmyoy the crooked church still clings to the hillside, supported by buttresses on all sides. Services are still held there and it continues to fascinate everyone who comes here.

At Llanthony the priory and the Abbey Hotel still offer a unique charm where the tranquillity and real ale are much appreciated after an evening's walk on the Hatterrall ridge. Fred would be pleased to see that the underground dovecote has been exposed and the remaining stonework pointed and preserved.

The little white chapel at Capel-y-Ffin is unchanged since Kilvert came here let alone Hando, but Father Ignatius's monastery now offers holiday accommodation and the Grange next door provides opportunities for pony trekking. In the ruins of the monastery church the grave of Father Ignatius has been restored and the walls of the building made safe so that entry is no longer a risk.

From Capel-y-Ffin the road leads on to the summit of the pass and then down the other side to Hay-on-Wye, renowned for its second-hand book shops. But do not come this way on a Bank Holiday for the traffic can be quite a problem.

Hay Bluff has become popular with hang gliding enthusiasts who soar above the Black Mountains and enjoy even greater views.

Ceiling boss at Llanfihangel Crucorney.

CHAPTER SIX

Around the wilds of Wentwood

Christchurch — Catsash — Penhow — Runston — Shirenewton — Llanfair Discoed — Foresters' Oaks — Newbridge-on-Usk.

From Caerleon Bridge drive past the Ship Inn and bear right to pass the King's Arms (B4236) to the top of Belmont Hill where a right turn will bring you to Christchurch.

Holy Trinity, Christchurch

The chancel is built on one of those "parcels" of Priory land owned by Eton College (transfered from the Priory to Eton College in 1536 by Henry VIII). I am informed that the Eton authorities after patient search, have discovered in the Forest of Dean the quarry from which the stone was cut for the original church and similar stone will be used for the rebuilding.

Since the fire, the church, beloved by us all, has stood open to the sky. It is possible now to get a clear conception of the original planning. Standing at the west end of the nave, observe how the chancel veers to the south.

Church authorities describe this "deflection of axis" as accidental, but when, in addition to many churches in our county I find great fanes like Cirencester and Stratford-on-Avon, the Norman church in the Tower of London, several of our finest cathedrals as well as many on the Continent, all displaying this feature, I can but say, "The nave was the body of our Lord, the transepts His arms, and the chancel His head, fallen sideways in death."

I am glad to record that the Norman archway, the "Healing Stone" of 1376 and the memorial known as the "Beauty of Christchurch" remain undamaged. Another monument of great interest to old Newport folk — the stone over the tomb of William Howe, skipper of the "Welsh Prince," which plied between Newport and Bristol — was, however, irretrievably damaged by frost during a recent winter.

The Beauty of Christchurch.

This fascinating L-shaped house known now as **Church House** adjoins the church yard at **Christchurch**. Thick grey walls on massive foundations support stout oak beams, which retain their strength after continuous use "from Elizabeth to Elizabeth," and some of the original windows remain.

Tradition ascribes the first house on this site to the monks of Goldcliff Priory. As if to support this, the tiny window in the south wall at the far end of the house looks directly onto the priory, four miles away, and it is pleasant to think that light in this window may have signalled "All's well" to the monks on the coast. But could such a light have been seen at such a distance?

Church House, Christchurch

During the first world war the chief-constable at Clevedon phoned to his colleague at Newport complaining that a light was visible at Christchurch. That light was traced to this miniature window, behind which a game of billiards was in progress.

The west wall nearest to the bus terminus, contains two lovely early Tudor windows, complete with interesting dripstones, two attic windows of the same period blocked up to evade the window tax, a large fireplace and chimney, and a portion of spiral stone staircase.

Facing the churchyard is a wall which runs the whole length of the house, and here is a veritable display of window construction. At the far end of the churchyard wall an external stairs led to the bedrooms. Another external staircase of oak used to beautify the south wall of the main building. In 1931, when the old house was threatened with restoration — please forgive me! — I sketched it in detail.

The existence of stables at Church House seems to show that it was at this house that the extra horses added at the King's Head Newport, for the Christchurch Hill ascent would be left.

We pass on the left the good stone house of **Mount St. Alban**. On this site, traditionally, the saint of Verulam was martyred. In Coxe's time a yew tree marked the position of the chapel dedicated to St. Alban, and in 1785 several stone coffins were disinterred. Alban's supposed shrine overlooks the Usk; from it you may see the summit of the Mynde at Caerleon, but an intervening bluff hides the ancient city.

Return via the top of Belmont Hill and follow the ridge road which drops down into Catsash.

The Farmhouse at **Catsash**, opposite the duckpond is the old inn, dated 1604. Here in coaching days, hung a sign showing a cat sitting on the branch of an ash tree. This was a pretty example of faulty translation for as Sir Joseph Bradney tells us, the original name was Cathonen, after a prince who ruled these parts. Villa Cathonen was a gift to the See of Llandaff in the Fifth Century, but by the Fifteenth Century it had become Cattesaishe and a century later Catche Ashe.

Throughout our land the inn and the church rub shoulders metaphorically. At Catsash the church adjoins the inn and, although it is now used as a barn, the decorated window in the east wall is still intact.

It seems that Catsash must have been administered by the Vicar of Langstone, whose church stands alongside the good road which you can see climbing the hill past Langstone Court.

You are now at Catsash, on the ancient main road through Gwent. Silures, Romans, Normans, Saxons have travelled along this ridgeway, reaching out westwards for trade or conquest.

From Catsash continue straight on through the hamlet of Llanbedr to join the A48 which will bring you to Penhow in about 3 miles.

Midway between Newport and Chepstow, on the left-hand side of the road, is a whitewashed farmhouse with outbuildings. It stands at the junction of the old coach road and the modern road, and almost opposite the lane to St. Brides Netherwent. This house was, until about 1868, the **Rock and Fountain Inn**, one of the most famous hostelries on the London road.

The "Rock and Fountain" at Penhow.

To breathe the atmosphere of old days at the inn I call on Mr. Charles Dutfield, aged 82, who was born at the "Rock and Fountain," and lived there until he retired 12 years ago from his post as surveyor. Mr Dutfield lives at "The Glen" in St. Brides, a beautiful gabled cottage draped with magnolia and wistaria, and the garden, on this calm, humid December morning, was fragrant with the scent of many violets.

I found Mr. Dutfield in this greenhouse, surrounded by carnations and primulas — a lovely setting for a talk of cabbages and kings, of education "then and now," of stage coaches and motor-cars, and of the "Rock and Fountain."

The old inn, it seems, was named after the castle crowned rocky hill of Penhow, and the fountain which gushes out into the meadow opposite. When the trade declined after coaching days, it ceased, in 1868 three years before the birth of Mr. Dutfield), to be an inn.

Sixteen horses were always kept in readiness in the stable at the "Rock" (seen at the right in my sketch). When the stage coach from Chepstow reached the Llanvaches pike the post-horn was sounded, whereupon the hostler at the "Rock" led out a change of four horses. This was also done at a similar distance to the west when the Chepstow-bound coach was approaching.

The bar at the "Rock and Fountain" was rendered attractive by the pretty bow-window facing the road. It was to this window, many years ago, that Mr. Dutfield led me, saying. "One of the small panes has writing cut into it which nobody has been able to read." Standing on the window-seat, and lowering the upper sash window, I leaned out and read the following, cut by a diamond on the outside of the pane:

Down in the valley come meet me tonight,
I'll tell you your fortune truly,
As ever 'twas told by the new moon's light
To young maiden shining as newly,
But, for the world, let no one be nigh,
Lest haply the stars should deceive me,
These secrets between me and you and the sky
Should never go farther, believe me.

September 23rd, 1820 *S.H.G.*

Outside the window was suspended a small bell, about eight inches high, which was rung to announce the imminent departure of the coach, when all the passengers hastened out, for the coachmen prided themselves on their punctuality.

I was deeply interested to hear Mr. Dutfield's memories of the old postman who had to walk with the letters from Caerleon to Llanfair Discoed by way of Catsash, Llanbedr, and the "Rock". He would then spend his time cobbling at Llanfair and walk back by the same route at night. It was impossible for him to call at all the farms and cottages, so he left the letters at convenient places.

For instance, people living on Grey Hill or "Money Turvey" would collect their letters at Mrs. Bladon's shop at the Pike in Llanvaches. Mr. Dutfield can remember letters remaining in the shop window for a week before being collected.

Phipps, the postman, was a shrewd old character. If a child waiting at the "Rock" for a pair of shoes said that his mother would send the money on the morrow, Phipps would say, "You can tell mother that if she sends the money tomorrow I will try and remember to bring them." The shoes would be in his bag the whole time, and would then be taken back to Caerleon, and brought back the following day.

Penhow Castle and Church.

Viewed from east or west, the crag of Penhow, crowned with castle and church is an impressive sight. During the last war artists among the German prisoners of war could be seen making studies of the hill, and one of them told me that it reminded him of his homeland.

"Pen" is the summit, and conjoined with the Scandinavian "how," gives us "the summit of the hill." There is evidence of Roman occupation on the site of the rectory near the church, and the strategic advantages of the hill commanding the prehistoric highway commended it to the Normans., Before 1271 the St. Maurs had built their stronghold on the hilltop. Doubtless the same family ("Seymour") founded the church.

In succeeding centuries the families of Penhow displayed great interest in the church. Sir Thomas Bowlais, father of John Bowlais who married Isabella Seymour, directed in his will of 1511 that his body was to be buried in the chancel of Penhow church, and left 40s. to pay for the "the beying of the bells".

Penhow church.

The original church, of the early English period, was the present nave and chancel. Tower and south aisle were a later addition. The tower was changed in 1840, during a ruthless restoration, from its old proportions to the present squat, pyramidal-roofed condition which strangely seems pleasant from below. In the tower are five inscribed bells, cast in 1744 by William Evans.

Near the entrance is the plain original font, big enough for a baby's baptism by immersion. The arcade is the work of several minds, one seeking complicated decoration, the others simplicity.

Original also, though re-surfaced in 1840, is the stone screen separating nave and chancel, while the chancel retains its double piscina and the recess in the north wall which once held an effigy probably of a St. Maur. Before this recess a light was kept constantly burning, provided for in the sixteenth century by the produce of one acre of land.

Out in the churchyard I found the tomb of "Roger Keene, Gent, of Penhow Castle," who died in 1830, aged 79 ā mere stripling in comparison with our own beloved Roger Keene, who also was born in Penhow Castle. The massive steps of the ancient churchyard cross surround now a venerable yew tree.

Venerable, too, was Elizabeth Tamplin, daughter of the vicar ofPenhow. She died in 1783, aged 111 years, having lived through seven reigns!

Continue along the A48 for about 5 miles to reach the village of Crick. Turn left here to follow the road to Shirenewton. Runston church is on high ground to the right and may be reached on foot from a right of way which starts near a farm (SO 494917).

The ruined church of St. Keyna, Runston.

We stood — the Bookman and I — on a hillock overlooking the Severn and Gloucestershire. The May sunshine enabled us to pick out the distant cliffs, Black Rock, and one of Mr. Enoch William's ferry-boats. Nearer, the trees of the plan displayed their new foliage, brighter than the green of the meadows. The Wyndcliff arose, pale blue in the east. All was peaceful, gravely beautiful.

Among the turf at our feet were many big stones, some flat with the turf. A big snake slithered across and disappeared in a hole, just as if the stones had swallowed it. Cool in the evening air, a thin wind whispered to us, "Runston, Runston, you stand in the dead village of Runston."

We were not the first to record the eeriness of **Runston**. Archdeacon Coxe saw it in 1800 by moonlight:

"The moon shone in its full splendour, affording light sufficient through the gloom of the surrounding trees, to examine the chapel... the roof was falling down, and the pavement was so slippery that I could scarce walk upon it without falling; a large and broken font was lying on the floor, among the weeds.

"The obscurity of this ruined sanctuary was broken only by the gleams of moonshine and the melancholy silence interrupted by the sound of my footsteps and the screams of the birds, which I disturbed from their nightly repose."

Half a century later those two good men of Gwent, Octavious Morgan and Thomas Wakeman, visited Runston in January to find masses of snowdrops among the ruins, indicating sites of former gardens once tilled by the smugglers, the sheep-stealers, and the poachers of the village.

Yes, the men of Runston were a disreputable gang. Unable otherwise to dislodge them, their landlords allowed the houses to fall into disrepair and somewhere around 1770 services ceased in the chapel, and the village died.

Services have not been held in Runston church since c.1770, and so I expected to find little of interest. Yet so strongly had the Twelfth Century masons performed their tasks that the chancel arch, the three windows, and the remainder of the walls retain their character.

The southern entrance, now piled up with bracken, was formerly square-headed, and surmounted by a semi-circular stone tympanum, whch was later removed to a neighbouring farm.

The chancel-arch at Runston Church.

Norman window at Runston Church.

Of the three windows in the nave, the one on the north, which I have sketched, is still perfect. The window aperture measures 2 feet by 6 inches. There are no grooves for glass, and it is difficult to imagine how the parishoners worshipped in such a dark and draughty temple.

There was no east window, and the chancel was lighted only by a small window on each side. The hole in the south wall of the chancel may have been for an aumbry or locker, but the large number of smaller holes throughout the building constitute a mystery. They are not putlog holes, for some are near the ground, but they may have been receptacles for timber on which other articles may have been fixed.

Tiny as it is — the total length is just sover 41 feet, not counting the belfry pier — this sanctuary has stood, a hilltop symbol of holiness for over seven centuries.

It was first mentioned exactly seven hundred years ago, in 1254, and in 1291 is referred to as Llangeneth — the Maiden's Church — the holy maiden being St. Kenya, daughter of Brychan, and sister of our own Gwladys the wife of St. Woolos (Gwynllyw).

In the same year — 1291 — Runston was included among those parishes which paid rent to Goldcliff Priory, and by that time all the land appertaining to the church ("Sladforlang") had been handed over by the Bishop to Robert de St. Pierre.

References to Runston occur at intervals throughout the centuries. As an example in the 1717 *Survey of Llandaff* we read that revenues of the bishopric were derived, inter alia, from *"the impropriate tithes of Runston."*

Then a curtain descends, and we hear no more of it until Coxe came by moonlight to the dead village, but it is cheering to know that an attempt will be made to preserve what is left of the little church.

The church of St. Thomas a Becket, Shirenewton.

Shirenewton is a pleasant destination. If we climb to it from the Cwm the embattled church tower resembles a hilltop fortress; from the Earlswood road with the Severn and Gloucestershire as background, the hamlet, embowered with trees, offers a charming welcome; and the gentle ascent from Crick bordered with pear-trees and blackthorn in blossom, and the steep hedge banks golden with cowslips and dandelions, tempts the visitor with the question, what lies hidden among all those trees?

Archdeacon Coxe took that last route in 1799, but reached only the dead village of Runston. Why he described Runston and neglected Shirenewton must remain a mystery.

Shirenewton has its roots deep in history. Its name takes us back to Durand who as sheriff held of the king a tenement in Caerwent called Caldicot. As Domesday (1086) put it, *"Durand vicecomes tenet de rege in careon j tenementum vocatum Caldecote."*

Shirenewton was the "Sheriff's New Town," but the Welsh in more poetic vein named it "Tre-newydd gelli fach" — the new homestead in the little grove. And in 1687 it was referred to as Nova Villa.

The church, dedicated to St. Thomas a Becket, was found by Humphrey de Bohun, Earl of Hereford, Constable of England, in the thirteenth century, not long after the canonisation of Becket in 1173. Among its rectors was our Adam of Usk, the great chronicler who in 1399 exchanged Shirenewton for Panteg.

A survey of the twelfth and thirteenth century church-towers in our county convinces us that the Normans thought it wise to combine worship with defence. Nowhere is this more evident than in that square tower of Shirenewton with its battlements and the windows, with the exception (obviously an afterthought) of the first-stage cinquefoiled lights, are defence slits. Four of these, by the way, are partly obscured by the clock-faces.

My choice of a northern view-point for my drawing was made to get the full effect of both sets of battlements, the square turret and the effective corbel-table below the battlements. The battered base of the tower I leave to your imagination.

I stayed awhile in the churchyard, savouring in the country quietude intensified by the music of thrushes and blackbirds. A stroll around the exterior, with its gargoyles, its king and queen on the label of the east window, its priest's door in the chancel, and its sheltering yews, prepared me for the rich experiences within.

Alas! A century ago, misguided enthusiasts, unconscious iconoclasts, removed from this splendid sanctuary most of the relics of old-time worship.

That there must have been a rood-loft is shown by the doorway beyond the chancel arch and the blocked doorway above the arch, but I could find no trace of screen or piscina. The big stoup in the porch looks forlorn in insecurity.

A north aisle added at the same time, stone heads — one of Becket — fixed on corbels in the chancel, and the arcading between nave and north aisle compensate little for the loss, in Bradney's understatement, of ancient character.

The porch with its upper room at Shirenewton Church.

Let us be content with that magnificent central tower, the nave and chancel, the porch with its upper chamber. Strange it is to note how writers have formed the habit of referring to these upper rooms as "parvises" — the term applied of old to the courtyard in front of a church or chathedral. Such rooms were used variously as schools, libraries, and even as stores for armour.

Until 1918 Shirenewton tower had five bells, and the inn opposite the church (now the village shop) was the Five Bells. All the bells were cast in 1756, when Great Britain declared war against France, when the "Black Hole" horror occurred in Calcutta, when the Seven Years War began. Yet one of the bells proclaims *"Peace and Good Neighbourhood, 1756."* The sixth bell was given by Captain C.O. Liddell in 1918.

Squeeze style, Shirenewton.

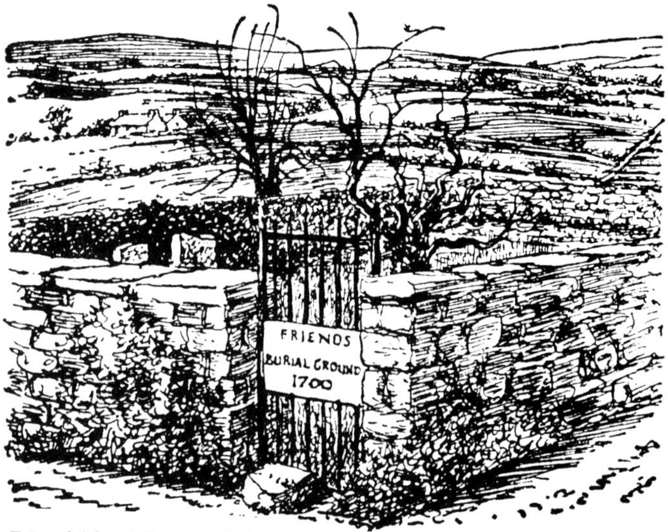

Friends' burial ground, Shirenewton.

The entrance to the churchyard above the memorial is a masterly effort in masonry. Half the steps reach out in semi-circles to help the visitor, while the upper half retreat in semi-circles to persuade him upwards.

I stop and talk to three of the stalwarts of the village. They tell me of the old days. They laugh when I ask why Shirenewton, so rich in pubs, had no school. "See what this so-called eddication does for you," is the comment as they point to a finger-post opposite the Cross Hands. I find later that the village is posted there as Shireneton.

The old post office, Shirenewton.

They tell of the village wheelwright, Tom Richards — how amid all his endless jobs he found time to cut and join his own coffin; how he was buried in the Friend's Burial Place.

I walk to that most evocative resting place and read, *"Friends Burial Place, 1700."* I place it in my memory with the Quakers' ground at Penygarn.

Now Mr. Benjamin invites me into his village home. A fine stone house it is, this "old post office," with its handsome central projection, its enormous external chimney, its attractive leaded lights. I calculate that there are 330 lights on the road front.

The date on ironwork is 1907, but the house without and within, bears evidence of great age; see for instance the "battered" stone bases to all the walls. Part of the stone roof survives, and the L in the six-pointed star refers to a family honoured above all others in Shirenewton.

Within the house I see the good spacious rooms. "It was a post office until some fifty years ago," says Mrs. Benjamin. "The postmistresses were the Misses Thirza and Lily Roberts; their brother John was the village postman. It was a busy house, for the well in the yard was the village well, and you can imagine how the news was collected and distributed there."

Behind Shirenewton church follow a road which passes the entrance to the lovely Cwm Valley and then on to the village of Llanfair Discoed.

The court-house, Llanfair Discoed.

Sheltering in the lee of Grey Hill the village of **Llanfair Discoed** takes its name from the little brown church which shelters in the lee of the castle. Visitors should not explore the castle (on private property) but view it from the meadows to the west whence the round tower gives still a frowning warning to the Welsh.

Inside the church porch is an inscribed stone which once was a stile into the churchyard. It reads:-

Who ever here on Sunday
Will practis Playing at Ball
it May be beFore Monday
The Devil Will Have you all

Near the church stands the inn, known half a century ago as the "War Office" because of the warfare located there when the Irish labourers employed on the construction of Wentwood reservoir called for refreshment.

Everywhere in Llanfair you will find the pink valerian, known to the villagers as "kiss-me-quick," and sweet smelling herbs. These with the tinkling stream which has come down from Grey Hill past the wayside well give the village an air of vernal sweetness.

At the junction of the two roads stand the Court House the farm and the pigeon house. With a window pattern of "1-5-4" and draped on the left by a big magnolia, the white facade of the Court House is striking and charming. If the magnolia blooms before its time a death is foretold — a superstition which I found in other villages of Gwent.

Above the porch is the Welsh inscription:

Eri fod yn ins maen dda yn wnc
1635

Six Welshmen have given me six different translations of this motto, but I choose as appropriate:

"Since it is small (i.e. the house) it is pleasant to be close together."

Opposite in the farmyard, is one of our most picturesque pigeon-houses, reminding us that of old, meat in winter was severely rationed, its place in the homes of the wealthy being taken by pigeon pie.

The pigeon house Llanfair Discoed.

Sir Nicholas, like Charles Hughes of Trostrey, fought for *'ye king against ye rebelles'*. In 1648 a band of royalists led by Sir Nicholas, and including Thomas Lewis of St. Pierre, William Morgan of Pembridge, and the fickle Sir Trevor Williams of Llangibby, attacked and captured Chepstow Castle.

After Cromwell had captured the town of Chepstow on May 11, Colonel Ewer proceeded to besiege the castle. With their provisions exhausted and their defences badly battered by gunfire the royalists troops offered to surrender and Thomas Lewis of St. Pierrre himself offered to give up the fight. Colonel Ewer insisted on unconditional surrender, and his demands were contemptuously refused by the gallant knight of Llanfair Discoed.

The end came soon, when the garrison left Kemeys to his fate and escaped through the breach made by Ewer's artillery. The attacking troops entered the castle and fell on Sir Nicholas and his few remaining friends who fought to the last.

Arthur Clark in *Chepstow: its Castle and Lordship,* quotes one report which told how Sir Nicholas Kemeys, *"A man of giant stature fought until he was disarmed, whereupon he was slaughtered in cold blood, his body dismembered, and portions of it cut up and worn in the hats of his killers as emblems of their victory."*

Up in the great wood the courts were held in the circle of oaks known as the Foresters' Oaks. The manorial courts were held in the Court House at Llanfair, while the date on the porch — 1635 — takes us back to the days when men were preparing to drench our fair land with their countrymen's blood.

Continue from the village up the hill and past Wentwood Reservoir to reach the Foresters' Oaks picnic site.

Wentwood — the "Fforest" of Gwent — extended from Christchurch to Chepstow. It separated Gwent-Ucha or Upper Gwent from Gwent Isha or Nether Gwent. When we add to that the other "Wentwood" (the name of which is preserved in manorial records), which covered much of Trevethin, Llanhilleth, Llanover and adjoining parishes, we see our fair land sheltered under a vast primeval forest.

The main Wentwood, composing originally seven thousand acres owned by the princes and kings of Gwent, became after the conquest a royal chase, famous for its beeches, hollies, yews and oaks. The ancient names of some of the groves, such as Cadira Beeches and Foresters' Oaks survive to this day.

When we decide to picnic above the reservoir we take either of the roads from Groeswen or Five Lanes. The junction of these roads is the apex of the triangle which forms our car-park and eating place — **the Foresters' Oaks**, six hundred feet above the Severn Sea shining silver to the far south, away over Alderman Tom Parry's beautiful reservoir.

To the left is Grey Hill, to the right "Money Turvey" (Mynydd All-Tir-Fach); we breathe in the upland air and the odour of the pines, and behind us is the steep hill which will take us down to the Usk with the glory of the Black Mountains at sunset seen through our windscreen. It is a god-sent place, this halting ground in our Delectable Mountains.

My drawing copied from a sketch made in 1839 by Mrs. Digby Wyatt shows two of the Oaks which may have been over five hundred years old.

Imagine a circle of such oaks. In their shade for centuries were held the foresters' courts. The jury was selected from the owners of estates who had by grants from the Lord the rights of house-bote, hay-bote, plough-bote, fire-bote, pannage and herbage. We talk of the royal chase of Wentwood, but all the power in the forest was vested in the lordship of Striguil (Chepstow) which was a lordship marcher.

The jury being empanelled, the vicar of Caerwent preached his sermon for which he received house-bote and hay-bote. Then the steward gave the charge to the jury, consisting of 25 articles, covering the interference with deer, martens, hares, foxes, eyries of hawks, bees or fish.

Article 25 reads: *"You are to enquire and present all suspected persons that hunt by night, or that carry any gun, traps or crossbows into the wood, or are found or taken in the manner of any of these four degrees, viz — Stable-stand, Dog-draw, Back-bearend, Bloody-hand."*

"Stable-stand" meant with bow bent ready to shoot, or concealed with a greyhound on leash ready to let slip. *"Dog-draw"* — tracking a wounded deer by means of a dog on lease. *"Back-bearend"* — caught in the act of carrying away the game on his back. *"Bloody-hand"* explains itself.

The hangman's oak on which the sheep-stealers were hanged, was the last to disappear, in 1903, while an adjoining field was within living memory called the goal-field.

Foresters Oaks, Wentwood.

The famous old oak on which the sheep-stealers were hanged no longer stands. It was of enormous girth and hollow, so that in its trunk four men could sit. The interior had been dried by the fires of countless tramps who had sheltered there, and one night about forty years ago it was found burning. A week passed before it was consumed, and many of the country-folk remember the red glowing pillar which gleamed so eerily against the blackness of the Forest. The site of the old oak is now marked by a coppice of young beech, while an adjoining field is still known as the Gaol Field.

The Forester's Oaks stand between two conical hills — famous landmarks — the twin hills of Wentwood. Their Welsh names are Mynydd Llwyd and Mynydd Alltir-fach, but we know them as Grey Hill and Money Turvey. From the road below the Oaks it is an exhilarating climb to the top of **Grey Hill**, and the views over the Channel and north to Wentwood are a reward for the exertion. Yet not one in a hundred who reach the summit knows that less than a quarter of a mile away lies a stone circle older than Stonehenge. To find it, walk eastwards along the ridge until you see a number of pits from which stones have been quarried. The circle may be seen immediately beneath.

Thirty-two feet wide, the circle is composed of recumbent stones, with no trace of tooling. Two standing stones with ridged tops rise, one to the north-east, and a further one to the north of the circle; a third menhir lies fallen within the circle. The two outer stones are in line with midwinter sunrise point; the north-east stone and the inner stone (when raised) would be in line with the midwinter sunset point, and there is a standing stone on "Money Turvey" on this latter line.

My theory is that when the ancient observers saw their stones in line with these horizon sunrises and sunsets they were able to advise their agricultural tribesmen that the seasons were. Such knowledge was power!

Mid winter sunrise on Grey Hill.

Leaving Foresters' Oaks follow the road up through Wentwood, past Cadira Beeches and Pen-y-Cae Mawr to descend on the other side enjoying magnificent views towards the Black Mountains. On reaching a road junction turn left for Llantrisant (previously visited) and after a couple of miles turn right to reach Newbridge-on-Usk.

The bridge and inn, Newbridge-on-Usk.

Memory chased memory as I stood in the middle "refuge" of the noble bridge. Handsome cattle from Whitehall Farm stood in the river, composing with the wooded hills a Highland scene which might have been painted by Landseer.

Upstream the river curled away under the bushes, and the hot summer sun robbed the hills of colour, veilling the more distant heights. Swallows dipped and rose above the stream, that same stream which had received us of old. "No man bathes in the same stream twice; no stream receives the same bather twice." So much change in the stream; so much change in the bathers. Yet today the river seemed unchanged, the hills and the bridge and the meadows held their old glamour, and my friends from half a century back — W.S., S.C.T., E.A.S., R.E.C. and a dozen more — murmured mystical greetings as I smoked in the "refuge."

The river crossing here dates from the dawn of history. In one of the legends of Cadoc the saint appointed three men to arbitrate in a quarrel between King Arthur and Ligessawe of the Long Hand. The king agreed to take a hundred cows, coloured in the fore part red, in the hind white. When these arrived at the ford of the Usk they changed to bundles of fern, hence the land near was called Tredunnock, the place of the ferns.

As the centuries passed a ferry service crossed the Usk at the ford. As early as 1295 the ferry, worth 10s. a year was a perquisite of the lord of the manor of Brethelly, which we know as Bertholey. Ruins of the old house are visible from the bridge; visible also are the ruins of the chapel of St. Bartholomew.

In 1521 John Thomas left 32s. 4d. towards the building — more probably the rebuilding — of a bridge. By 1776 the wooden ruinous bridge had fallen, and three years later when the arch of the new stone bridge was nearing completion two of the builders and a boy were swept down the river by a sudden flood, the men being saved, but the boy drowned.

Archdeacon Coxe was in a better position than we are to record who built the present fine bridge. It is pleasant to think of the old builder of Pont-y-pridd as the builder of Newbridge, and of his son, David Edwards as the builder of the Newport bridge of 1800.

From here the return route to Caerleon is made via Tredunnock and then there is a choice of the lower road through Glen Usk, the ridge road via Llanhennock or dropping down to follow the old main road from Usk to Caerleon.

EDITOR'S NOTES

Christchurch was burned down on the night of November 5th 1949. It was subsequently restored at a cost of £45,000 and completed in 1955.

At Catsash the peace is now disturbed by the noise of traffic speeding through a great cutting below the village on the A466 which connects the Coldra (M4) with Monmouth.

The hill top castle at Penhow has been opened by Stephen Weeks, a film producer, as a tourist attraction. Claiming to be Wales' oldest lived-in castle, audio tours are offered in four languages. The castle has been beautifully restored and every year a return visit is worthwhile for there is always more to see. At the time of writing, the owner is also restoring the old Rock and Fountain Inn and turning the site into a heritage centre to be operated in conjunction with the castle.

A few miles away the tiny church of Runston has been made safe and the stonework pointed to prevent further decay. This work was carried out some years ago by the Department of the Environment and the building is now in the care of Cadw.

Shirenewton is always a pleasant destination with the Tredegar Arms serving several real ales, but I wonder how Fred managed to miss the "pirate's grave" in the churchyard — a slab of stone bearing the well known symbol of the scull and crossbones.

Llanfair Discoed is unchanged apart from housing developments but at Foresters' Oaks there is now a Gwent County Council picnic site with car park, toilets and a waymarked trail leading to the summit of Gray Hill and the prehistoric stone circle.

On the other side of Wentwood at Newbridge-on-Usk the scene is still tranquil but the inn has undergone many changes and has recently been revamped yet again.

CHAPTER SEVEN

On the Wentllwg Levels

Tredegar House — St. Brides — Marshfield — Bassaleg — Peterstone — St. Mellons — Castleton.

Starting at Bassaleg follow Forge Lane (A4072) down to the M4 (Junction 28) and turn left along the A48. At the next roundabout turn right to follow the B4239 past Duffryn School and housing estate and turn right for Tredegar House Country Park.

"Morgan" said my Welsh friend and mentor, is one of our most evocative names. "Morgan" — and he lingered over the vowels — "song of the sea."

It is almost within earshot of the song of the sea that the ancestral house of the Morgans stands **(Tredegar House).** The park stretches thence to Bassaleg, undivided by a road, for the Newport-Cardiff road ran through Bassaleg. It was sheltered on the north-east by the Gaer hill, and bordered by the waters of the Ebbw, dashing seawards "with pebbles in his throat." It is land which was never bought or sold, remaining in the same hands through recorded history.

Tredegar House. The north-west facade.

Imaginative bards traced the origin of the Morgans to the third son of Noah. I shall be satisfied with Cadifor-fawr, an eleventh-century chieftain of Dyfed, eighth in descent from whom was Llewellyn ap Ifor, lord of St. Clear.

Llewellyn married the most beautiful lady in the land, Angharad, daughter of Sir Morgan up Meredith of Tredegar — the lady whose skin was of the hue of drifted snow" — and her son was

Ifor Hael the patron of Dafydd ap Gwilym. In the poems of the great bard we learn that Ifor was not only a warrior, but that he loved the chase, he loved his people, he loved poetry. How like his descendant, who endeared himself in his many-sided personality to us all.

In 1448, Sir John of Tredegar was a knight of the Holy Sepulchre. His son, Sir Morgan of Tredegar, was knighted on Blackheath field by Henry VII, himself a Welshman. It is this Sir Morgan who engages our immediate interest, for it must have been he who began, and perhaps completed (for he lived until 1504), the Old Hall, which is shown in my drawing.

This was the hall of the "faire house of stone" noted by Leland, and has come down to us little changed. The beautiful early Tudor windows of four and five lights, surmounted by double dripstones, fill the white room with light, while the fireplaces — one of the same period as the windows, the other Elizabethan — suggest that the Morgans demanded warmth as well as light.

The temperature was in the lower twenties as I walked along the drive towards Tredegar House. Snow lay on the lawns, the rhododendrons, and the branches of the splendid trees, and the swans seemed "dithered," as we say by the ice on the lake — that lake where his lordship used to catch trout for his guests.

During recent years the house and grounds have been taken over by St. Joseph's Covent. School was in session, but the Reverend Mother, with great kindness, found a viewpoint from which I could sketch the Old Hall (now the refrectory), and then faced the Artic conditions without in order to show me the memorial to "Sir Briggs." There she left me within a circle of yew trees to sketch the monument.

Memorial to Lord Tredegar's charger, "Sir Briggs".

In my drawing, the obelisk is merely suggested, and the details of costume, saddle etc., are as I saw them on the monument. (I cannot agree that I should display in my illustrations an exact knowledge of uniform and equipment when I am representing memorials which have been worn by time or damaged.)

While it is poignant to compare the horse and rider in the splendid painting still to be seen at Tredegar House with the stone monument portrayal, my cold heart was warmed as I read the noble tribute from a man to his horse.

There is a most touching sequal. A beautiful canvas in the house shows "our" Lord Tredegar nursing a Skye terrier. That little dog was buried near Sir Briggs and I found his memorial surmounted by a broken column. With difficulty I deciphered the inscription:

"In loving memory of Peeps
fondest and most affectionate
of Skye terriers, who died
Sept 6, 1898.

His honest heart was all his master's own
There are some both good and wise who say
Dumb creatures we have cherished here below
Shall give us joyous greetings when we reach the golden gate
Is it folly that I hoped it may be so?"

The Reverend Mother then arranged for me to see every room in the house. Guessing correctly that I should have lost my way in such a three-storeyed labyrinth, she had requested Sister Mary to act as guide, and Sister Mary undertook her job with the gay spirit of an Irish colleen.

We were accompanied by my son Robert, and a handsome Scottish Border collie named Prince, who was more interested in mice than in Morgans.

The north-eastern porch, with its spiral stone pillars and balcony surmounted by the stone lion, gryphon and reindeer, opened into the entrance hall, panelled in oak from floor to frieze. Over the fireplace we saw at once Charlton's painting, "The Charge of the Light Brigade," with Captain the Hon. Godfrey Morgan — "our" Lord Tredegar — as its central figure, borne boldly and well into battle by "Sir Briggs".

Adjoining the entrance hall on the right was the diningroom, converted now into the chapel. This lovely apartment, panelled in oak, contains the arms of Morgan on windows and ceiling, and above the splendid fireplace, a quaint old painting of "Lot's wife."

"You will notice," remarked Sister Mary, "that it is Lot, and not his wife, who is looking back." She showed us the altar and altar-rails, both converted from a Tudor bed, and when she opened the old serving hatch we found the walls to be 2ft. 9 in. thick.

The great staircase was of particular interest to us, for Sister Mary had seen an ancient parchment, since destroyed, which stated that the magnificent balustrading had been carved from the timbers of a galleon which had belonged to Sir Henry Morgan the Buccaneer.

We moved now into a most impressive room, where the exuberant splendour of Restoration days was combined with perfect proportions. Above and below the great wall-panels, and round the fireplace, scrolls and wreaths were carved. At intervals amid the sumptuous display, busts of emperors and goddesses looked down on us. This was the room, 42ft. long and 27ft. broad, which Coxe saw in 1800, when he was informed that the floorboards (which run the whole length of the room) had been produced from a single tree growing in Tredegar Park. The ceiling of this "brown room" — now the music room — like the ceiling in the diningroom, was reconstructed a century ago.

On the walls of the music room are the portraits of the first viscount, nursing "Peeps," a characteristic painting of Evan Morgan by Ambrose McEvoy, and canvasses showing Sir Charles Morgan, his eldest son and his beautiful wife, Mary Margaret, whose monument at Bassaleg portrays her with her seven weeping children.

Of equal worth is the Gilt Room, now the art room. Here the girls of the Convent High School are taught by Sister Mary under the only original ceiling, surrounded by allegorical paintings around the upper walls, and amid the dignity and stateliness of 1674.

The influence of Grinling Gibbons is evident in the proportions and the carving. We wondered what old Sir William Morgan, enshrined between the twisted columns above the resplendent fireplace, would have thought of the glory with which his portrait is surrounded — that glory which would have proved so fine a setting for the King's visit to Tredegar.

The portrait of Sir William Morgain (aged 90 in 1650), like almost all the Morgan portraits, displays the same fine features and the same appearance of calm command that we associate with their gallant descendant, the first viscount.

While we were examining the Gilt Room, Sister Mary pointed to some scratches on an upper window pane. We deciphered the name "William Morgan," and a date which may have been 1681. This must have been scratched on the glasss by the son of the old civil wars veteran whose portrait we had studied above the fireplace.

Continue along the B4239 following a pleasant road to reach the small village of St. Brides.

"Bends for half-a-mile" brought me within sight of **St. Brides village** and soon, in the teeth of the north-east wind, I was sketching one of the most beautiful church towers in Gwent.

In spite of its buttresses, the tower is not upright, but "the pull of the sea" cannot be blamed, as the leaning is towards the land.

St. Brides Church.

High on each side of the tower, bisecting the battlements and graceful parapets, is a stone figure under a canopy, and I wish it were possible to tell you whom they represent. I am tempted to ascribe the impressive seated figure on the west side to St. Bridget herself but an older figure appears halfway up on the south side.

The top of the stair-turret shows hexagon-shaped, above the battlements, and the whole tower, with its grey stones silvered by the morning light, is a joy for ever.

Above the porch someone has fixed the scratch-dial stone, and above the porch archway is inserted a window which is much older than the porch. Alongside a carved head on the inner wall of the porch is the famous tablet which records the height of the "great flud" of 1606.

St. Brides church was far too spacious and cold for its small congregation, and so the nave was divided into two portions by a wooden screen which reaches to the ancient roof timbers. As far as I could tell the roof timbers, which seem to be original, are in good condition, and when the bosses and corbels were enriched with paint and gilding the roof must have been an impressive sight. There are still signs of the rood loft fixtures and a piscina in the south wall of the chancel.

Chilled by my sojurn in the churchyard I made my way to the beach, and stepped out briskly along the sea wall. Here, my friends in the salt-laden wind and the bright sunshine with the seagulls screaming overhead, here you may find the tonic you need after a winter huddled over the fire.

And if that does not suffice, try a hurried dip in the waves as they come racing in over the mudflats. Maybe it was over those mudflats that St. Bride came ashore. Do you remember her legend?

St. Bridget was the pure and stainless Virgin of Kildare in Ireland. When she refused to wed a wild chieftain of her father's choice the old man threatened to force her into the marriage, whereupon the saint caused her eyes to drop out on to the ground. Her father shrieked and fled.

Calmly Bridget took up her eyes, washed them, and made her way to the seashore. Here she cut sods of turf, and using them as boats, floated across the sea to Cambria, where she is remembered in the many churches dedicated to St. Bride.

Continue along the B4239 and take the second turning on the right to reach Marshfield where a loop road may be followed to the church which is well concealed in a circle of trees.

Few churches in Monmouthshire have had as much loving care lavished on them as **Marshfield**. As I approached it from the village I stopped to admire the view of the western tower set amid the ring of Wellingtonias. These great fir trees sprang into favour in Monmouthshire about eighty years ago, and they are picturesque in the grounds of mansions like Brynglas and Hatherleigh.

Nowhere else, however, were they planted in a ring as at Marshfield where until recently they have grown undisturbed. The onset of disease now makes it necessary to cut down alternate trees at once, and the remainder later. They will be replaced by a type of cedar which is not allergic to salt breezes. The trees mark the line of the ancient fence. In the church register the vicar showed me an entry for 1720 recording a parish meeting to discuss the churchyard fence which needed a repair.

"Ancient and substantial" inhabitants described how of old the fence was "equally allotted and divided in parcels adapted to each tenant" who was then required to maintain and repair his portion. It was then resolved to proceed according to ancient custom and divide the 1,230 feet of fence equally among the sixty tenants, except for *"a gate or set of rails leading from the lane by Alice Roberts* (? church cottage) *and the other leading from the lane by the pound."*

The south-eastern boundary of the village pound is still marked by an upright inscribed stone in the churchyard, and in the churchyard near the south porch is the stump and base of the village cross which doubtless stood of old at the crossroads where the houses named Croesfach and Croesfawr were raised.

Marshfield church in its circle of firs.

Most of the stone used in Marshfield church is our own red sandstone, and it glows beautifully in the light of the setting sun. With few exceptions, the restoration of Marshfield church has been a splendid example of inspired and scholarly work.

The story of this reconstruction and decoration tells how in the early years of the nineteenth century one service only was held on Sunday, when the psalms were read in English and the rest of the service in Welsh. The church was in a sad state of disrepair, and there was but one communicant — a poor bed-ridden woman.

Then Sir George and Lady Forestler-Walker led the parishioners in a determined attempt to restsore the beautiful but neglected church. Repairs to the damp walls and the erection of the reredos, the east window and the wellingtonias date from these bright years; the organ replaced the western-tower musicians in 1883. Eighteen years later the porch was rebuilt, the old cheap roof removed and the present oak roof with its heraldic decorations giving the church history from 1135 (together with the instruments of the Passion) raised in its place.

The bells were recast and rehung, a new floor laid, a full sized baptistry (for baptism by immersion) built into the aisle, and church lamps were replaced by gas, the generating house for which was erected in the churchyard.

Among the parishioners who took part in the restoration were the rich, who contributed their thousands, the poor gave proportionately, and *"two non-conforming gentlemen who expressed their willingness to pay shilling rates towards the restoration."*

Return to the B4239 and continue to Peterstone.

As I surmounted the railwaybridge at **Marshfield**, the coastal plain of Wentloog lay bathed in the morning sunshine. Straight towards the sea stretched the silver reen, and straight alongside, gleaming like pewter, ran the road.

I paused to imagine the view on January 20, 1606, when the Severn Sea overwhelmed the plain, and the people of the plain took to their rooftops. This morning, however, all was serene.

Serene, that is, except for the howling north-easter. Mocking the sunshine, it spread across the plain, bending the treetops and sending the smoke from the cottage chimneys in flat wisps, whilst the birds above Marshfield trees wheeled and dived in ecstatic aerobatics.

The tower at **Peterstone**, seen from any standpoint is noble. Have you ever stood on Gray Hill and taken a bird's eye view of the churches on the Caldicot Level, or on the so-called Roman road for the view of the Wentloog churches?

Peterstone, the church and the inn.

From Portskewett to Nash, from St. Brides to Rumney they stand, sentinels guarding the coast, while across the waters a similar line of towers echoes the pattern, and the most impressive of all the Monmouthshire coastal towers is St. Peter's.

You may see Peter himself in a panel on the north side of the tower, accompanied on the other sides by St. John, St. James and the Virgin and Child. The sculptured figures are of the same style as three of the four on St. Brides tower, and both towers have small western doorways.

Approaching the church, I noted the inscription on a stone at the north-east corner:

THE GREAT FLOOD
JANUARY 20, 1606

The leaded mark of the inscription is 5ft. 6in. above the ground.

In the pinnacled porch I found again carved heads of royal, angelic and holy aspect. Within the church I got the same impression of white light that forms my vivid memory of Nelson's church at Burnham Thorpe.

The clear light and the aspiring arches at Peterstone — especially the arch leading to the tower — have an invigorating and uplifting effect, and I cannot imagine any worshipper sleeping there during a sermon.

Each roof corbel holds a face. None of the faces is classical or stylised. As at Magor and elsewhere in Gwent, they seem to be portraits, and if that is so the present inhabitants of the village are more photogenic than their ancestors.

Stone stairs leading from the north aisle to the rood-loft have at their base a piscina, and that is unusual. A second piscina is in the south aisle, a third in the chancel, and signs of the removal of the rood-loft remain on the chancel arch. There are eight bells in the tower.

The first church at Peterstone appears to have been built by Mabel Fitzhamon, daughter of the Norman Robert Fitzhamon, in the early twelth century.

Among her gifts to the Priory of St. Augustine, Bristol, was the monastery of Peterstone, and thenceforward, until 1539, the prior was the rector of Peterstone.

At Peterstone I felt the pull of the sea. Soon I was passing the field known of old as "Cae Bull," the place of bull baiting, and also the site of the Bull Inn, the licence of which was transferred to the Six Bells.

Much work had been done to repair last winter's inroads into the sea wall. In the process I fear, the tiny hovel of "Betty the Fish" has disappeared. Betty, you may recall, collected her fish and walked with them in a basket on her head from Peterstone through Marshfield and Castleton to Cefn Mably in time for breakfast. I discovered an excellent painting of Betty hanging in the great hall at Cefn Mably, and that I fear, is the sole relic of the tough little Peterstone fisherwoman.

Back in the village I called to see the extension to the **Six Bells**. On a previous visit I had sketched the magnificent fireplace with its lintel-beam 13ft. long. Stone stairs in the thickness of the fireplace walls of the main house were lighted by the window seen in the gable end. The gigantic beams and joists combine with the fireplace and stairs to endow the bar with a genuine late sixteenth century atmosphere.

Now the Six Bells has six dormers, for the cottage has been incorporated. This had two rooms

on the ground floor, but the partition wall has been removed and an axial beam twenty feet long, six inches wide and one foot deep is now seen with its accompanying joists.

"To reach the bedrooms," I was informed by a knowledgeable native of Peterstone "they climbed from the rear room up a steep ladder-stairs. At the front of the cottage were the mounting-stone and the milking shed." I was unable, however, to solve the problem of the two recesses, low in one of the walls.

Upstairs, in cottage and inn, the roof-timbers bore evidence of one carpenter's skill. Throughout the bedrooms the principals, generally 1ft. 6in. deep, were sustained by crucks which resembled arch-braces, unusual in my experience. On both floors the necessary restorations have been made with skill and good taste.

The fireplace at the Six Bells, Peterstone.

There is a tradition that the Six Bells was once an almshouse. Its propinquity to the church, like the Six Bells at Newport and scores of other "church houses," suggests that one of its functions was to supply the ale for the frequent church feasts and another to house travelling priests.

It was with pleasure, that on leaving the shelter of Peterstone church I encountered Mr. Rees, who scorning the bitter north-east wind, invited me to accompany him to the sea wall.

"I had hoped," I protested, "that you and I would sit over a cosy fire while you talked to me of Peterstone."

"What is the use of that?" he asked. "I want you to see the things I talk about."

I begged him to don an overcoat and muffler, but he refused, saying that he was of a tough breed. God bless him! He was tough in truth, this Harry Rees of Peterstone. As a boy he spoke no English, and now how he speaks no Welsh, yet the old Welsh names survive in and around Llanbedr Gwynllwg (Peterstone).

They are nearly all colour names, like Heol Las (green lane), Bryn Glas (green bank), Ty-Gwyn (white house), Ty-coch (red house), Ty-glas (blue house); the long reen is Rhosog Fawr (the great stream of the marsh), and the Horsecroft Reen and Broadway Reen join to form Gout Fawr (The great reen exit).

Mr. Rees pronounced "gout" as "gut", which tempted me to connect it with the local term for a tail, but I am sure that, just as "don"is "do on," and "doff" is "do off," so "gout" is "go out."

"In this field to the east of the church," said Mr. Rees, "are the ruins of a monastic building, and beyond that field my fathers as a young man helped to demolish a great wall 90ft. long, 9ft. wide and 9ft. deep. Was that the end-quay of a canal leading from the sea?"

It is certain that sea-trade took place between Peterstone and Bristol. It is also worthy of note that a cottage to the west of the church is called "Anchorage," traditionally the terminus of a canal, but that is I fear, scant evidence.

As we walked seawards I asked Mr. Rees why such a large church should be found in so small a village. His answer was certainly surprising.

"The sea wall ahead of us — at least the clay wall — was raised by Nicholas Chapman, who lies in the church. I believe that in the old days the parish extended to another wall now far over the mud flats."

"Over there, pointing to the south east, "I came across a cemetry with about 25 graves, the bones still lying in the clay holes."

We walked eastwards on the sea wall. I asked him how they shopped in Peterstone seventy years ago. He chuckled: "You with your cars, don't know what shopping can be."

"Many's the time I've walked to Marshfield for a ha'porth of barm for baking, and to Castleton for a loaf. And the post came only once a week. All the letters were left at the Six Bells, and each family collected its own post."

Still beating to the windward we came to a little bay "Now you can see the cut stones," exclaimed Harry, "and here, I believe, was the entrance to the canal, if such a canal existed."

This was what was left of the small port of Peterstone. Into the bay empties Gout Fawr, and the wall on the right is still called the New Quay. The wall along which we walked is Peterstone Great Wharf. It was fascinating to imagine the little ships sailing from this little bay to the world-famous port of Bristol with their cattle and farm produce, but I imagine that the tiny harbour offered meagre shelter in the winter gales.

Leaving Peterstone follow the B4239 for about 3 miles and then turn right again to reach St. Mellons where the village is split by the A48.

I parked my car near the "Fox and Hounds," (in pretty **St Mellons**) crossed the road, and immediately left this mad century to find the homes and church of a more gracious age. Around cobbled courts the pretty cottages gathered, each bearing its own characteristics of form and decoration. The people who live in these cottages are serene and good-tempered, pleasant to the stranger, and happy in their surroundings.

The vicar was busy mowing his lawn but with no hesitation he left this job half-finished, and devoted the next hour to the stranger. He had come to St. Mellons from the three-fold parishes of Llanarth, Bryngwyn and Llansantffraed to find his new church sadly in need of repair. Already the essential repairs are well in hand.

This church is dedicated to St. Mellon. According to one authority, this saint, also referred to as Melo or Melanius, was born at Cardiff, became Bishop of Rouen, where he built the first cathedral in A.D. 270, and planted Christianity in Gwent. "Llaneirwg" — the Welsh name for the church — may refer to the complexion of Malanius; it is more probably a reference to a saint named Lleirwg.

There is a tendency to discredit the story of Melanius, Bishop of Rouen. No student of history, however, will deny the connection between South-east Wales and North-west France, a connection which continued throughout the Dark Ages. Three centuries after St. Mellon's days the powerful monastery of Llancarvan was ruled over by an Irish monk named Brandan.

A lady of Gwent, on pilgrimage to the monastery, gave to the world a son, whom Brandon named Macout or Malo. Obeying the order of God — I am here translating from the French record — who wished him to admire the marvels of creation, Brandan and his "moines-navigateurs" set out on voyages of exploration. Malo, now a young man, accompanied Brandan, and at the end of seven years of wandering, and encountering all manner of dangers. Brandan died in the year A.D. 578, possibly in Jersey.

Visitors to St. Malo should make the short sea trip to the island of Cezembre, where stands to this day the oratory consecrated to St. Brandan of Llancarvan — the oratory visited by the maidens of the mainland, who never fail to knell in the grotto to beg from St. Brandan the blessing of a good husband!

St. Mellons Village.

The church of St. Mellons, as I found on that July afternon, has a dignity and an atmosphere all its own. This partly explained by its proportions, partly by its splendid "cradle-roof," partly by its unique plan.

The main entrance was at the base of the tower, but this entrance was unfortunately changed into a window, and the main entrance blocked, the south porch taking its place. Strong and square, needing no buttresses the embattled tower seems to command from its hill-top the coastal plain, with outposts of Christianity at St. Brides, Peterstone, Marshfield and Rumney.

There is no suggestion within of nave and aisle lay-out. The whole church is 105 feet long, the nave opening by one arch into the chancel,, and by another and smaller arch into the north chapel. A large "squint" enabled the occupants of this chapel to see the priest at the altar.

The south chapel has two arches opening into the nave and one into the chancel but the carved clusters of foliage and grotesque heads were removed from the roof of this chapel into one of the restorations.

There is some good glass in the windows of St. Mellons, but why is a reredos of foreign stone (quite out of place here) allowed to obscure the lower portions of the east window? I should like to see here an oak reredos, in scale and in tune with the excellent screen.

With the fourteenth century windows (and one of earlier date), its wonderful roof, its Fifteenth Century tower and porch, its beautiful lych-gate, its organ, and especially its position overlooking the channel, St. Mellons Church holds a unique place in the annals of Christianity in Gwent.

Did not a Bassaleg farmer once offer to bet me a half-a-crown that the "Roman" road above his fields was a hundred years old if it was a day?

In most instances these mounds were raised by the Normans, and certainly 'Cas-bach' (Castleton) must be related as Mr. John Kyrle Fletcher pointed out, to the "castles" of Maesglas and Rhymney . If we take Maesglas and Cas-bach, they are singularly alike. Neither mound shows any trace of masonry, but notable residences were built near both, the house at Castleton being owned in 1497 by John Kemeys, coroner of Wentloóg, and the house of "Maisglaise" in Leland's time by Henry Kemeys, "a man of means."

The mounds, therefore were thrown up by the Normans as their first attempts at the defence of newly-occupied territory. Any dwellings would be in the nature of a "keep" on the mound until more peaceful conditions permitted permanent dwellings, and these became incorporated, at Maesglas, into the farm-buildings now demolished, and at Castleton in the modern "Wentloog castle."

From St. Mellons continue along the A48 to Castleton where the Wentloog Castle Hotel is on the left.

Entering the grounds of **Wentloog castle**, I was welcomed by a host of daffodils shining under a noble cedar. The lawn which had suffered so much during the war was now fully recovered and the house —which had suffered more — was again its old gracious self. Camellias bloomed in the conservatory, and the sunshine was beatific.

My charming hostess, Australian-born, has more than her fair share of zest. Like most from the dominions she was anxious to soak her mind in the lore of the motherland, and I was astonished and delighted to find how well-informed she was about her adopted county. and what taste she and her husband had displayed in the restoration of the house and grounds.

Wentloog Castle and mound.

We climbed to the top of the castle-mound seen on the left of my sketch. A prettier castle mound I have never seen, for primroses and anemones and crocuses peered out from among the rhododendron bushes.

The view from the summit commanded Wentloog and the channel on the south and our oldest road on the north, and the temptation is of course to connect this defensive mound with the prehistoric camps of Coed Defaid and Penylan and the great monolith at Druidstone.

Now many a hamlet in our land has its "castle" or "tump" without any sign of masonry. Often the villagers will ascribe such a mound to the Ancient Britons or the Romans, and I fear that their historical time-sense is not over-developed.

On reaching the roundabout by the M4 at Junction 28, turn left up Forge Lane (A4072) and return to Bassaleg. From St. Mellons continue along the A48 to Castleton where the Wentloog Castle Hotel is on the left.

On the lynchgate in the centre of Bassaleg, where church and chapel folk, may read it, is the beautiful war memorial erected "to the honoured memory of the men of Duffryn Graig and Rogerstone. They were as a wall unto us by night and day. 1914-1919."

The noble figure above, standing against a gold mosaic background, was the work of Mr. Gilbert Bayes.

Near at hand is the Tredegar Arms. It was in 1854, when the son of Sir Charles Morgan, of Tredegar House was fighting in the Crimea, that George Borrow came to Bassaleg, having walked from Caerphilly.

"I soon reached Bassallaig," he wrote. "A pleasant village standing in a valley and nearly surrounded by the groves of Sir Charles Morgan. Seeing a decent public house I said to myself, 'I think I shall step in and have my ale here, and not go running after Sir Charles Morgan, whom perhaps, after all I shouldn't find at home.'

"So I went in and called for a pint of ale. Over my ale I trifled for about half an hour then paying my groat, I got up and set off for Newport."

The *"decent public house"* was undoubtedly the Tredegar Arms and although Borrow did not know it. Sir Charles Morgan's gallant son was fighting at Inkerman on the same day that Borrow had climbed Phynlimmon!

Come into the "Morgan chapel" with me. Read the inscriptions on the mural tablets, then stand before the exquisite "Adoration." When you have filled your soul with its beauty and grace, examine the figures in the four niches. Here is a bishop, here is a saint who may be St. Basil, there is a king, but at the foot on the right is an officer of the 17th Lancers.

Incongruous, you feel, to see him in such company? Not to us, for this is our own Captain Godfrey Charles Morgan, who rode on "Sir Briggs" in the Charge of the Light Brigade at Balaclava — our own Lord Tredegar.

Very truly he belonged to us. In our school days we held — we still hold — that Tennyson inhabited Parnassus. As we roared out the poem our hearts beat in rhythm with the hoof-beats of "Sir Briggs" as he road into the mouth of hell.

While we grieved over the slain we rejoiced that our own hero had been spared, had lived into old age, so that we might know him. To see him in the flesh after all this hero-worship was no anti-climax. The slim, alert, well-poised figure, the steady, clear eyes, twinkling as he passed on to us one of his epigrams, the air of quiet command coincided with our own image of him.

The famous old charger, "Sir Briggs," which had carried his master boldly and well at Alma, Balaclava and Inkerman, was buried in the grounds of Tredegar.

One of the wags of those days spread the legend that the horse was buried in the tump of Twyn Barllwm and none chuckled more heartily than his lordship when the legend reached him.

Lord Tredegar remained with us, identifying himself with every worthy cause until 1913, when he died aged 83. Who can say how many sons of Gwent were inspired by his memory in the wars that followed?

EDITOR'S NOTES

St Bride's Church is now in a sorry state for the tower is leaning at a strange angle and the church is no longer used for services.

The village of St. Mellons has been expanded with the construction of a large housing estate on the south side. Fortunately the tremendous volumne of traffic that once passed through the centre of the village has been reduced by the extension of the M4 motorway. The village boasts four pubs which are all in close proximity; the Fox and Hounds, Bluebell Inn, White Hart and The Star.

Marshfield Church is still impressively ringed by tall trees giving the appearance of being in the middle of a wood. The tall Wellingtonias form a semi-circle around the church to link with five large 'conker trees', but opposite them is a short gap where some of the old Wellingtonias were cut down. Adjoining the church is a new vestry which has recently been constructed in stone and it blends in very satisfactorily with the old church.

Wentloog Castle is now a busy hotel belonging to the Ladbroke group. Extensions have been built on extensions and in complete contrast to the old building, accommodation is provided in a nest of concrete cubicles. The lawn mentioned by Fred is now a large car park and the castle mound covered in rhododendrons may be ascended by a flight of steps which provide access to the "Castle Garden" on the summit.

Tredegar House is no longer occupied by Sir Joseph's School for that has moved to a new building nearby. This noble red brick mansion was purchased by Newport Borough Council in 1974 and has been carefully restored and refurnished. The surviving 90 acres of parkland have been opened as a Country Park and special events are held there during the summer. Outbuildings have been converted into craft shops, a bar, restaurant and visitors centre. In May 1987 a circle of Gorsedd stones was erected in the grounds as part of the parparation for the National Eisteddfod which is to be held here in 1990.

CHAPTER EIGHT

Exploring the Caldicot Levels

Nash — Goldcliff — Whitsun — Redwick — Undy — Rogiet — Llanfihangel Rogiet — Sudbrook — Portskewett — Black Rock — Mathern — Llanmartin — Bishton — Llanwern.

A complicated grid of tidal ditches named reens drains the sea-moor. "Reen" is an ancient water-word, derived from the same roots as Rhine, Rhone and Rhondda ('good water'). But the reens have with one exception Saxon names like Bowleaze, Saltmarsh, Gout and Elver Pill. "Gout" is pronounced "gut" and is the expressive name applied to the exits, beyond the sluices of the reens.

Most impressive of the reens is Monksditch. From its head waters in Wentwood, past Tregarn mill and the Ford farm it flows until at Llanwern it is raised eight feet above the road level and continues thus to Whitson and the sea. The monks of Goldcliff Priory performed this remarkable feat of engineering.

I have vivid memories of boyhood days alongside Monksditch. My father's passion for eel-pie took him and us, to the great reen, and while he fished we enjoyed the fearful thrill of emulating Blondin, crossing and re-crossing the narrow tree-trunks which spanned the reen. Yet we never mustered sufficient courage to pole-vault the reens, as the farm-labourers did with their "powts".

I have know Monksditch in the depths of winter, when the high winds whistle through the reeds; I have seen, on a still summer evening, a heron, unaware of my presence for minutes, standing as if in meditation in the cool water; but for magical loveliness give me the banks of Monksditch near Great Barn in February, when the snowdrops nod to their silver reflections.

Human habitation of the sea-moors goes back to remote ages. We have as evidence the Iron Age landing camp at Sudbrook, a Stone Age communal tomb and a Roman villa site near Portskewett, Roman relics from Redwick and Goldcliff, and a "stone of hope" maen gobaith — a guiding stone beyond Magor alongside the old road which crosses the plain from Sudbrook to Christchurch, where it joins the prehistoric and Roman ridgeway.

It is a mistake to talk of Caldicot Level as "devoid of Welsh place-names". Recall Lliswerry, Llanwern, Pwllpen (Pulpan), Craig-y-Perth wood, Pant-yr-Eos, Spytty (Yspitty), Bryngwyn, Llanfihangel Rogiet and especially the sonorous Llancadwaladr at Bishton, Nash of course is "an ash", its Welsh name being Trefonen.

From the Coldra Roundabout (M4 Junction 24) follow the A455 past the Ringland housing estate to turn left at the third roundabout and then past Nash Technical College, to soon leave the traffic behind and follow a country road. To reach Nash take a right turning.

On a grey morning I was driving homewards from Goldcliff. Ahead of me Newport lay under a pall of cloud and smoke. Suddenly the sun broke through from a southern cloud and shone like a searchlight on the tower and spire of an ancient church. Forgetting the highway code and all other mundane affairs, I pulled up short to see this mysterious manifestation from heaven.

It was a view which would have set Turner or Constable aflame. The grey stone steeple, strongly stereoscoped against the sky gloom, glowed with a silvery radiance: the flat meadows were enamelled a vivid Irish green: the sheep looked up, startled by the sudden brilliance and I felt as Moses must have felt when he stood before the burning bush.

In such moments of transfiguration the beauty of this county of ours is so exquisite as to defy expression by word or line: it demands the "cold purity of music".

Nash church

West of the church arose two stacks like the funnels of an enormous liner. I thanked the gods of Gwent that our biggest generating station had been placed here, at Uskmouth, instead of at Llanover, but a sudden prophetic vision showed me **Nash church** in A.D. 1970 lost in a wilderness of brick and mortar, concrete and stucco. So I set to work to record it in its pristine setting.

The sketch completed, I took the turning marked "Uskmouth", and found the hedges in late October, laden with the big blackberries which we usually pick in mid-September.

At the bend of the lane I came within sight of the church, known hereabouts as the Cathedral of the Moors, although the people of Magor and Peterstone give the same name to their churches.

Nash church belonged to Goldcliff Priory in 1349, when Robert Arney was instituted to the benefice. I wonder what the original builders would say to the misguided folk who have maltreated this stately old sanctuary. They would call down maledictions on the vandals who removed the stone mullions from the windows, replacing them by timber mullions from a village school; the four boars' heads on the tower snarl at the chimney on the porch (now turned into a vestry).

Within the church there is the same evidence of cheap nasty treatment of the House of God. Nash is, I believe, the only Monmouthshire church to retain its original box-pews, three-decker pulpit, and musicians' gallery. Yet somebody with the soul of a cockney cheapjack has daubed thick paint on this priceless ancient furniture.

At a close view the tower and steeple retain all the grace which I had admired across the meadows. Where the spire springs from the tower the other ugly change in comformation is screened by a charming pinnacled stone balustrade.

Buttresses support the tower and the nave on the north side, so "the pull of the sea", (see Whitson) must be reversed here. A mark on the tower indicated the height to which the flood rose in 1606. As at Whitson there is a scratch dial on the south wall of the nave.

Big as it is — and there were congregations of four hundred during the war — Nash was originally much larger, for the west side of the tower indicates that there was once a north aisle. The axis of the chancel diverges southward from the nave axis.

When I visited Mr. Herbert Stevens at Manor Farm, Whitson, he described a terrible storm in the early years of this century. At the height of it a neighbour ran to tell him that a ship was wrecked off Nash Lighthouse.

"We collected other men living near," said Mr. Stevens, "and made our way to the lighthouse. The tide was going out and soon we were able to reach the wreck. One drowned sailor lay on the mudbank, the other four — the crew of a Bristol trader laden with general cargo — were lashed to the mast, all dead. We carried them and laid them on the floor of the bellringers' room in Nash church tower."

Now when I returned the church key to Mr. Cornelius Cox at Church Farm, Nash, I asked him if he remembered the tragedy.

"Remember it?" he cried. "It was my job to ring the bell for evening service and that I did standing among the five corpses. I still think that they might have done for once without the bell."

Return to the original route and follow the signs to Goldcliff village.

Goldcliff Church.

In **Goldcliff village**, church and inn, as usual rub shoulders. The approach to the church is under an avenue of pollard limes, on which a few leaves were still hanging at my last visit. To the left is the tower with its simple battlements, to the right the chamfered base and stump of the churchyard cross.

Over the porch is the sundial, inscribed *"C.W., 1729,"* the gnomon springing from a jolly little stone face. Within the church all is white and plain and I felt here as at Nash that it would be good to see the stone-work rid of its plaster defacement. I note with pleasure that the vicar, who ministers already to Whitson and Goldcliff, is to take over also the splendid church of Nash.

The inn is known variously as the Farmers' Arms, the Dealers' Den and the Gluepot. In front is a semi-circular hedged enclosure around which, at closing time, the farmers run nine times, to keep themselves fit. So I was told.

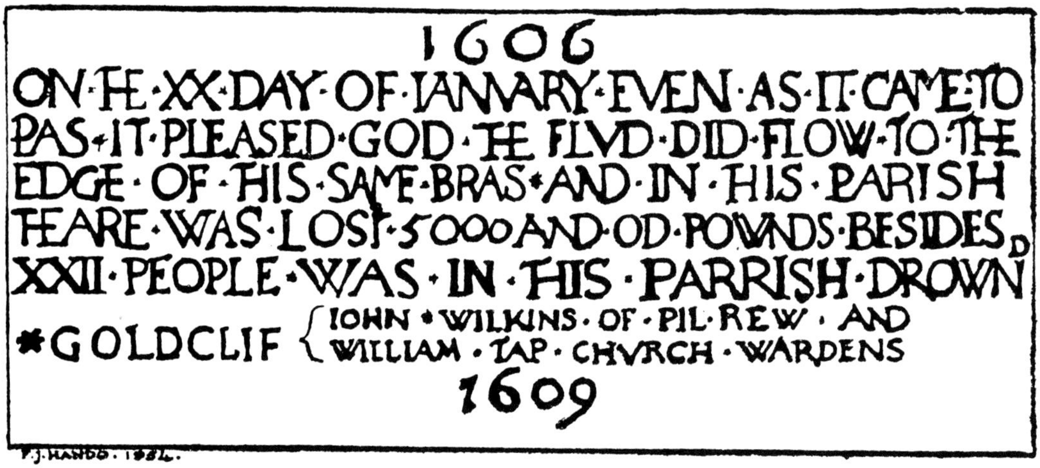

On the north wall of Goldcliff church, 2ft. 3ins. above the chancel floor, is fixed a brass measuring 7¾ins. by 3¼ins. As my copy shows, this was one way in which John Wilkins and William Tap, churchwardens recorded the terrible flood of 1606. The other way was their presentation of plate, paten and chalice inscribed with their names and the date 1609.

My readers will note the attempt on the part of Messrs. Wilkins and Tap to render their record in poetry; they will note also, that the twenty-two people were second in importance to the "5,000 and od pounds".

The date 1606 is the same on the porch inscription at St. Brides across the river, which breast high reads:

THE GREAT FLUD
20 JANUARIE
IN THE MORNING
1606

A hole five feet above the ground in the embattled porch of Redwick church is accompanied with the inscription: GREAT FLOOD. A.D. 1606. Yet, in the next year, 1607, a tract, *"printed for W.W., to be sold in Paules Churchyards at the sign of the Grey hound,"* had this title:

"Lamentable newes out of Monmouthshire in Wales, contayning the wonderfull and most fearefull accidents of the great overflowing of waters in the saide Countye, drowning infinite numbers of Cattell of all Kinds, such as Sheepe, Oxen, Kine, and horses, with others; together with the losse of many men, Women and Children, and the subversion of xxvi parishes in January last, 1607."

On the title page is a lively woodcut which I have ventured to copy. Above the surging floods arise a church steeple (is it Nash?), two cottages and two trees. The tree on the left supports a

1607 Woodcut.
"The Great Flood".

beared man and a boy sitting in the forks and another boy at water-level. On the right hand tree sits a fully-clothed man (with tall Welsh hat) and a boy who is naked except for his nightcap.

One of the cottages is untenanted, but on the roof crest of the other sits a tall-hatted man with his hands raised in prayer. Three other figures with night-caps stand or swim in company with horses, cows, an ass and a sheep.

The address to the reader which opens the tract begs him to observe how God had punished the victims of the flood and urges him to "look into his own courses" lest similar or worse fate might befall him. The theory seems to be that the sinful suffer misfortune while the sun shines on the righteous!

Then the description begins with:

Woeful newes from Wales

or The lamentable losse of divers Villages and Parishes (by a strange and wonderful Floud) within the Countye of Monmouth in Wales; which hapenned in January last past 1607, whereby a great number of his Majesties Subjects inhabiting in those partes are utterly undone."

This section is printed in handsome black letter, somewhat difficult to read. Six pages of further exhortation follow. Then comes a reference to the damage wrought in Somersetshire, where *"ye sea got up between Barstable and Bristowe at high as Birdgewater,"* the whole of Brent marsh being covered. Then, at last we come to the account of the flood in Monmouthshire, where the following 26 parishes were *"spoyled by the greeuous and lamentable furie of the waters: Matherne, Portscuet, Calidcot, Undye, Roggiet, Llanfihangel, Ifton, Magor, Redwicke, Gouldenlifte, Nashe, Saint Peire, Lankstone, Wiston, Lanwerene, Christchurch, Milton, Bashallecke, Saint Brides, Peterstone, Lambeth, Saint Mellins, Romney, Marshfield, Wilfrick."*

Over an area of moors 24 miles long and 4 broad, all kinds of cattle were drowned, ricks and mows of corn were carried away, a multitude of houses were beaten down, *"scattering and dispersing the poore substance of innumerable persons"*, causing damage to the value of £100,000.

After four more pages of homily, we read of the speed of the incoming waters: *"no Greyhounde could have escaped by running before them,"* covering *"the richest and the fruitfullest place in all that Countryey."*

A man and woman marooned in a tree saw a *"certaine Tubbe of greater largenesse"* approaching. Committing themselves to the tub, they were carried safely to shore.

On this bitter January morning a mother, seeing the waters approaching, placed her four-year-old daughter on a beam. A little chicken running before the waters flew up alongside the naked child and by its warmth preserved her life.

Poor Mistress Van, whose house was four miles from the seawall, was drowned before she could get up into the higher rooms of her house and her living, mark you, was an hundred pound and better by the year.

A multitude more than the estimated *"twentie hundred"* might have perished from hunger and cold had not Lord Herbert and Sir Walter Montague sent out boats, conveyed for ten miles on wains to relieve the distressed.

The author ends his tract with this prayer: "The Lorde of his mereie graunt, that we may learne in time to be wise unto our own health and salvation, least that these water-flouds in particular prove but fore-runners unto some fearful calamaties more generall."

Continue for about a mile and then turn right to follow the road down to the sea wall.

Standing sixty feet above high tide, **Hill Farm** is the successor of the famous **Goldcliff Priory** and some of the cut stone in the farmhouse especially the lintel of the cellar entrance, may have been part of the priory buildings.

Long before the foundation of the priory the centurion Statorious with his Roman cohort built a portion of the sea wall and inserted the stone which cleared up in 1878 the mystery of the building of the wall.

Before the masonry was added to the base of the "hill" it was possible to see the reason for the English name "Goldcliff" or the equivalent Welsh "Allt Eurin". From the sea the cliff was limestone above and red sandstone below and in these lower strata were shiny particles which some authorities named as mica and others as pyrites.

Goldcliff Priory was annexed to the abbey of Bec in Normandy whence a prior and twelve Benedictine monks came to Goldcliff and to the monks of the priory we can assign with fair certainty the establishment of the salmon fishery and the construction of that amazing reen known as Monksditch.

The priory buildings arose between the present farmhouse and the sea. In those summers when we knew long weeks of sunshine the grass turned brown in rectangular patterns on the hill. These patterns were over the ancient foundations and must form a tempting site for future excavations.

Roots of oaks and an abundance of hazel nuts found on the sea-flats at low tide indicate that a forest grew south of the priory. Similar discoveries, 45ft. below the surface, were made when the Alexandra dock was being cut across the river.

It seems likely that in addition to the priory Robert de Chandos created the manor and parish of Goldcliff, dedicating the church to St. Mary Magdalene. When the alien priories were suppressed Goldcliff was annexed to Tewkesbury Abbey, but the Welsh would have nought to do with the new monks and drove them out, imprisoning the prior in Usk. After a further attempt at settlement it was granted in 1451 to Eton College, to Tewkesbury in 1461 and to Eton in 1468. At the Dissolution the gross value of Goldcliff Priory was £2,898.

The priors at Goldcliff lived at times not a wholly cloistered existence. In 1334, it seems, Phillip de Gopillarius the prior was charged with a monk, some clergy and fifty other persons from Newport, Nash, Goldcliff, Clevedon and Portishead with stealing wine and mechandise from a vessel wrecked at Goldcliff.

In *Commons & Customs* we read how in 1784 a party of smugglers landed at Goldcliff 12 hogsheads of tobacco weighing 9,804 lb. and a cask of brandy containing forty gallons. These goods were found by the customs officers in a farm outhouse and taken to Newport under armed guard *"as the country is full of smugglers and inhabited by a desperate set of people."*

Two months later at Goldcliff there was a further seizure of 130 gallons of rum and brandy. And in 1833 the schooner Kate of Bristol, landed at Nash Point 252 kegs containing about 1,100 gallons of brandy which were found by the customs officer in an otherwise empty house.

On my visit to Goldcliff I met by great good luck Mr. Ralph Burge and his son, the proprietors of the fisheries. They invited me to inspect their sheds and stores and here I was able to see actual putchers and the "fore-wheel" of a kype.

Mr. Stanley Stuart Gifford (who I later met in Newport) confirmed that the taste of sturgeon was reminiscent of veal and added the interesting information that when Eton College owned the priory property, one day annually was devoted to sending sufficient Goldcliff salmon to satisfy the whole college.

Did the Romans, who built twenty miles of sea wall between Sudbrook and the Rhymney, fish at Goldcliff? So far we have no evidence, but I fancy that the centurion Statorius and his cohort (who fixed the inscribed stone six feet below the present level of the green "wharf") found Severn salmon a welcome addition to their rations 1,600 years ago.

And I am quite certain that the salmon had something to do with the siting of the priory on "the hill". What sumptuous repasts those monks must have enjoyed on Fridays!

Return to the last road junction and keep straight on to shortly turn right for Whitson. Park by a gate on the left to follow a path leading to the church.

Whitson Church.

At **Whitson** we inspected the church. As my sketch shows, the tower leans southwards, drawn in that direction, I was told, "by the pull of the sea".

At the top of the stair turret is the "thimble tower", which the villagers aver was placed there to prevent any further seaward leaning. The big tower window leans considerably in the opposite direction. Great baulks of red sandstone form the quoins of the tower.

Passing an interesting scratch dial in the south wall, we entered the porch. Here, again, was further evidence that the ancient church builders at Whitson had no passion for symmetry, for the right-hand column of the inner archway stands on a stone base, while the left-hand column, without a base, is three inches shorter. Above the left-hand column is still visible the beautifully carved consecration cross.

The church consists of nave and chancel, separated by a sharply pointed chancel arch, while the chancel axis slews southward from the nave axis. The big, solid-looking font is Norman, while the silver chalice is of 1575, when the vicar was David ap Gwilym.

The large bell in the tower is inscribed "God save our King and Kingdom, and send us Peace. W. and E. 1758." and the small bell of the same date: "Obedite.". On the walls are memorials to the squires of Whitson Court, who are buried in the tumulus-like vault in the churchyard.

Return to the main route and turn right to follow the road past the long Llanwern Steel Works and follow the signs to Redwick.

The church of St. Thomas the Apostle, Redwick.

Redwick owes much of its character to the complicated system of reens which drain its meadows. Each reen has its own name and you may find in the Redwick district the following reen-names:

Oxlease, Greenmoor, Gabber's Gout, Bowleaze, Bareland, Stutwall, Waun Deilad, Longlands, Monkscroft, Brassgout, Decoypool, Coldharbour, as well as the more expected Hare's Elver Pill, Crabtree and Village Reens.

The church of St. Thomas the Apostle at Redwick is worthy of study. A hole in the porch five feet from the ground shows the height reached by the devastating flood of 1606. This moorland church contains one of our few remaining rood-lofts and screens, and as my sketch indicates, the chancel axis bends northwards from the nave axis. It was interesting but not surprising to find that in the east window Our Lord is shown with his head fallen in death to the north.

Rood-loft in Redwick Church.

Stone steps wind up from the south aisle to the rood-loft, whence the door on the right opens to a further flight leading to the bell-ringer's room in the tower. It was in this room, some years back that an eerie affair occured which explains why Redwick folk do not play cards.

On the last night of the old year, the ringers were assembled in the loft awaiting the death of that year and the birth of the next. They latched the door and, to while away the time, decided on a game of cards.

As the cards were dealt the door flew open. The dealer closed and latched the door and dealt the cards, when again the door opened.

"Summat's gone wrong with that there latch," he observed as he closed, latched and bolted the door. Again he shuffled the cards, but as he dealt the first card the door burst open! Now crazy with fear the ringers staggered down the steps and into the cold bleak night. The old year died and the new year was born, unheralded by the bells of Redwick.

Redwick Church had a narrow escape in the last war. Three bombs fell on the night of August 5, 1942, on the field next to the churchyard and if the German airman responsible for that attack reads these lines, maybe he will tell us what military objective he expected to destroy in Redwick.

From Redwick continue to Undy.

St. Mary's Church, Undy.

Approaching **Undy** I saw the little brown church stereoscoped against a golden southern sky, the gold reflected in a lake over which flew scores of seagulls, This lake was of course, a flooded field, one result of the inordinate rains.

Undy may be "Gwyn-ty" — the white house — but that is only a guess. We hear of it first, inevitably, in the survey of Wentwood of 1271, when Sir Bartholomew de la Mare had housebote and haybote at Undy. The manor was held in 1314 by Gilbert de Beauchamp, and in the sixteenth century by Lewis of Van. Another manor in Undy owned a fishery on the Usk from Caerleon to Kemeys Commander.

The church was a handsome structure until 1878, when, to use a sweet understatement of Sir Joseph Bradney, it "suffered a severe restoration", including the removal of the central tower. I noticed again at Undy the determined way of churchwardens to secure immortality, this time by a deep inscription on a stone in the porch.

CW
R J 1790

The great bell in the turret, the thirteenth century work in the south entrance and the chancel arch, the Norman font and the chalice of 1577 remain.

Norman font in Undy Church.

The first reference to Undy was in the sixth century, when Gwyndaf Hen was the principal of the college at Caerleon, following the death of Dubritius. He and his wife it seems, founded the church at Undy which was dedicated to them.

The ancient names of the village, Gwyndaf, Gwyndi and Wyndaf, seems to confirm this story and the corruption thence through Woundie and Wondy to Undy is explained.

Three strangely parrallel lanes come south to the Severn. The first, through Magor and across Whitewall Common ends at Magor Pill; the second climbs over Vinegar Hill, passes through Undy and ends at Chapel Tump and its farm. The third comes over Common Coed (where, I believe, it is called Nanny-goat Lane) and "fizzles out" near Collister Pill.

Three similar lanes may be seen, like cricket stumps — balls complete — north-west of Caldicot, while the amazing N.W.-S.E. lanes in the Forest of Dean, almost geometrically parrallel, have never been explained.

After the Conquest, Undy remained in Welsh hands until 1240 when Pembroke and St. Maur took it. In the survey of Wentwood, 1271, Sir Bartholomew de la More had houseboot and heyboot at Undy. In 1314 the manor was held by Giles de Beauchamp, again in 1391 by a St. Maur while in the sixteenth century Squire Lewis of the Van (near Caerphilly) bought it.

On a cold windy afternoon I stood contemplating the floods and the moors and I wondered why these old land-grabbers were so anxious to acquire Undy.

Bradney gives us a list of tenants in Undy during Cromwell's protectorate. The names include Harbert, Probert, Morris, Essington, Rosser, Addams, Young, Blethin (later the bishop), Walter, Thomas, Coles. Many of these names survive on the moors.

The vicar of Undy accompanied me as I drove over the railway bridge. St. Mary's Church, seen against the floods, resembled the churches which I remember in the Norfolk Broads.

"These floods," commented the vicar, "seem at first to subside quickly, but a residue pool survives sometimes for years. The church, as you see, stands above flood-level on a strange promontary of rock which lies beneath the surface."

Seen from the churchyard gate and stone stile, the church bears obvious signs of unsparing Victorian reconstruction.

"Our unique bell, cast in Bristol between 1350 and 1380, inscribed 'Virgini Marie Lavdes' was housed before the rebuilding in a central false tower. However, you will find that much of interest has survived," said the vicar.

Some of the stonework in the lower portions of the "battered" walls was original and I am quite sure that the primitive stone heads which act as finials to the label over the western door were part of the original fabric — as was the doorway itself.

The buttresses to the south walls suggest that the promontary on which the church was built provided less security than was expected.

On the attractive south porch is inscribed:

C.W.
R. J. 1790 4

– another example of weakness in numeration reminding me of the tombstone inscription to a "baby aged 101 years" — the only way the mason knew of recording "eleven years"?

Within the porch are stone seats and a good Norman doorway leads into the bright church where I was immediately engaged in careful study of the Norman font. My drawing shows the steps, columns and square font, but my eyes caught sight of a cavity in the rim and when I lifted the cover there was a similar cavity opposite.

My memory flashed back to similar cavities in the font of a church in Jersey where I was instructed that they were for salt and oil. Salt and oil were used in the ancient "baptism" ceremonies. Salt, says the Oxford Dictionary of the Christian Church, induced Christian wisdom, perserverence and integrity; oil ensured the fulness of sacremental grace and the gifts of the Holy Spirit.

By a strange coincidence the chalice of St. Mary's, Undy, is dated 1577 and might be one of the dozen chalices distributed to churches in this diocese, according to tradition, by Queen Elizabeth. In St. Mary's Risca, as I recorded, the chalice is inscribed "Risca 1573".

The church registers date from 1760 and the church-wardens' account books include many a quaint entry. An example is: "1807. Ink and paper for five years, 6d. Thomas Jones, C.W."

Soon after leaving Undy turn right along the B4245 and look out for a standing stone in a field on the left, just before reaching Llanfihangel Rogiet.

On my journey to **Rogiet** I stopped between Magor and Llanfihangel Rogiet to examine a standing stone in a big field to the north of the road. It is seven feet high, five feet wide at the base and over two feet thick — it is known locally as "the Devil's Quoit".

The Devil's Quoit.

In a charming letter written at Buenos Aires, Mrs. Lynette Wood tells me this legend:

"Our Lord and the Devil were standing on the top of Gray Hill arguing whose strength was the greater. The Devil picked up a stone and threw it into the Long Field beyond Putcher's Field; our Lord, picking up a larger one, threw it into the Channel, hence the Denny."

The story which I was told long years ago was that the Devil had hurled this quoit from across the Channel. The same story is told of a similar stone found near the opposite shore.

It seems certain that the Devil and his confederates must have spent much of their unholy time throwing great stones about our land, for you will find his stones and his "arrows", Giant's Hurlers, Giant's Throws, the Hag Stone of Moll Walabee and Devil's Quoits flung for vast distances.

In Monmouthshire our own beloved rascal Jack o' Kent, after jumping from the Sugar Loaf to the Skirrid, took up three vast boulders and tossed them fourteen miles to Trellech where you may still see them.

"The Devil's Quoit", is a typical "maen gobaith" (guiding stone), directing along one of our oldest roads. I am told that efforts made to remove it have failed, but if they had succeeded, dire consequences might have befallen the offenders, for under the ancient laws of Wales a man's life was forfeited if he removed a "main gobaith".

The ruined windmill at Rogiet.

From the Quoit I drove to the windmill on a hill a hundred feet above sea-level north of Rogiet. I have been at fault in describing "our only windmill" the one at Llancayo, and in addition to these two there must have been a third on Christchurch hill which is mentioned in Civil war correspondence and a fourth near Redwick.

As I returned to the main road Vinegar Hill rose ahead and soon turning right along the old, old road I came soon to the break in the hedge which gives that superb view of **Llanfihangel Rogiet** church, set amid the picturesque outbuildings of the court. I shall not forget this midwinter scene, church and trees silhouetted against the morning sky.

The name Llanfihangel (St. Michael's church) is found usually on the hilltops of our land. Seen from the road, this church of the moors justifies its name for it is on a slight eminence. Llanfihangel Rogiet implies the joining of two manors when Robert Gamage, of Rogiet, married the daughter of John Martel of Llanfihangel.

In common with so many other churches near here, Rogiet church has changed its dedication. Originally St. Hilary's — named after Eleri, an eighth century Welsh abbot — it is now dedicated to St. Mary. The graceful slender tower is surmounted by pinnacles and (to my delight) a "thimble tower" like the one we noted at Whitson, (see page 147).

Llanfihangel Rogiet Church.

At Whitson, you may remember, I was instructed that the "thimble" was erected to counteract the pull of the sea. Unfortunately for the theory, the thimble at Rogiet is on the south east.

"When I was a boy," said Mr. Bob Anstey, "a thorn was growing out of the thimble. Archdeacon Bruce was the rector — you may see his grave with a reclining cross near the porch — offered ten shillings for the removal of the thorn.

"I well remember a young fellow, supported by a rope around himself and the thimble, edging around and around and at last cutting away the bush."

Within the church the most imposing relic is the tall, narrow arch, leading from the nave to the tower. Remains of a holy water stoup near the door, the stairway to the rood loft, the altar slab, the ancient font and the chalice inscribed "Ecclesia de Rogiet 1625", have survived.

It will interest the people of this lively and enterprising village to know that in 1869 Rogiet contained eight houses and 36 inhabitants.

Continue along the B4245 and just beyond Caldicot turn right for Portskewett.

There are three relics of Norman workmanship in **Portskewett** church, and in the churchyard to the west is the traditional site of the palace where Harold entertained Edward the Confessor.

We know that Harold, helped by Norman mercenaries — one of whom, John Scudamore, he placed in charge of the Saxon tower at Kentchurch — conquered parts of South Wales.

Then, according to Caradoc the Welsh historian, he built a magnificent house at Portskewett and filling it with great quantities of provisions splendidly entertained the king.

Portskewett Church.

Smitten with envy and jealousy, Harold's elder brother Tostig staged a stupid scene at Windsor for which the king forbade him the court. Wild with fury, Tostig rode to Hereford, where Harold had another palace and many servants were preparing a sumptuous entertaiment for the king.

Tostig's villains lopped off hands and legs of some, arms and heads of others and threw them into the butts of wine and other liquors, charging the surviving servants to acquaint the king, "That of other fresh meats he might carry with him what he pleased, but for sauce he should find plenty ready provided for him."

Harold's house at Portskewett was demolished by the Welsh under Caradoc ap Gruffydd, who bore away "all the costly materials which had been brought thither to beautify and adorn the structure".

Turn right by the church and follow the road to Sudbrook.

Sudbrook camp has always exerted a powerful influence over me. Only half of its embankments remain, for the sea has engulfed the rest. The camp was old when the Romans came, as Dr. Nash Williams has demonstrated, and there is no doubt about its purpose. It was constructed to guard the Porth-is-Coed — the port below the wood — Wentwood.

Where was the port? Where was the harbour? The Welsh Triads describe it as one of the three great ports of Britain and the evidence of the learned and dependable J. G. Wood, F.S.A., is of great assistance to us. Writing in 1914 he avers:
"Seventy-ton barges floated up St. Pierre Pill upon the tide half-a-mile above the viaduct and used as late as 1860 and within my own recollection, to lie up to discharge coal for St. Pierre House. It was no doubt at one time tidal nearly to the point where the Roman road crossed it at New Inn" (at the foot of Pwllmeyric Hill). *"This would be a mile and a quarter further upstream."*

This harbour was the estuary of the Mounton Brook, which nearer the sea is named Pwllmeyric Brook. In the old days, when the volume of water was considerably greater, it was enough to work Linnet Mill, Lady Mill and Lark Mill at Mounton.

In 1846 Brunel built a viaduct a quarter of a mile long over the Pill, and this was replaced in 1860 by an embankment which has since borne the railway traffic. A glance at the ancient maps of Monmouthshire confirms J.G. Wood's account of the estuary.

"Porth-is-coed" — the name of the harbour — became also the name of the manor, which extended from the harbour to the South Brook (Sudbrook), and also of the village quite a mile from the harbour (Portskewett).

Mr. Wood concluded that St. Pierre Pill and Sudbrook Pill were harbours dating from Roman times and that the crossing from the end of the Via Julia at Avonmouth was either to St. Pierre Pill or to Sudbrook Pill, both guarded by Sudbrook Camp. It is safe now to state that the Porth-is-Coed was in use in pre-Roman times.

The ruins of Holy Trinity Church, Sudbrook.

On Saxton's map ***"Trenytie Chapel"*** is shown just to the east of Sudbrook Camp and as I stood and sketched the ruins of this little church I became aware of a trinity of men's works which spanned the centuries. The camp at least 2,000 years old and the church, at least 700 years old, were cheek by jowl with the Severn Tunnel pumping station, not yet eighty years old.

There is no great charm in the grey ruins of Holy Trinity, Sudbrook. It is difficult to account for its erection here, unless it was a private chapel for John Southbrooke, who is mentioned in the Wentwood Survey of 1276.

As I walked around the ruins and stood on the edge of "Trinity Cliff" I recalled that Octavius Morgan, in 1858, gave us the names of some of the rocks and sandbanks near Sudbrook: *"Bedwin"*, *"Cruggy"*, *"the hillocks"* and *"the fortified hills"* are surely folk memories of an inhabited land suddenly swamped by the Severn Sea.

And at an inquiry in 1758 was there not a witness who swore that he had mown grass on Charston Rock, which was then joined to *"the continent"*? All this seems to point to a bigger parish for Holy Trinity than we envisage today.

Holy Trinity at Sudbrook was in use, it seems, to the end of the Eighteenth Century. Bradney tells us that one of the last to be buried there was Captain Blethin Smith of Sudbrook, who left instructions that his corpse was to be borne to the grave by six seafaring men.

Return to Portskewett, turn right and after about 1 mile turn right for Black Rock.

On a calm, damp November morning I stood on the sward at **Black Rock** and watched the receding tide laying bare the rocks and sandbanks. Through the smoke of my pipe I saw in fancy the old-time ferryboats crossing to and from Gloucestershire.

Black Rock.

Stout cutters they must have been, like the old Newport pilot-boats, flying on fine days a mainsail, a top-sail, a foresail and a jib, but on windy crossings, a double-reefed mainsail and maybe a storm-jib.

In the autumn of 1798 and 1799 Archdeacon Coxe and Sir Richard Hoare *"crossed into Monmouthshire by the new passage. The breadth of the Severn ... from the inn on one side to the inn on the other is three and a half miles ... we passed near a rocky islet ... well known by the appellation of Charston Rock. The stone (from the islet) is highly esteemed for its durability, and was later employed by the architect of Newport bridge for the lower part of the piers. I disembarked at the Black Rock and ascended to the inn."*

A century and a half earlier, on the 23rd July, 1645, thrills were a-plenty at Black Rock. Prince Rupert had crossed and made his way to Bristol the night before and it was confidently expected that the king would follow him, in spite of the fact that a party of Cromwell's dragoons was known to be in the district.

The King did not appear, but according to one account a party of Royalists from Crick crossed from Black Rock in safety. On their return the ferrymen were met by a group of the enemy, who forced the sailors to take them across.

The boatmen, all loyalists, landed the soldiers on the "English stones", a sandbank joined to the Gloucestershire shore at low tide, as it was on that occasion. As the cutter turned northward for home, the tide began to flow strongly and the soldiers were all drowned.

This "new passage" is quite clearly the link which connects the Via Julia of England with the Roman roads of South Wales.

Throughout the centuries the ferrying of passengers continued either by this route or by the Beachley-Aust route, or by both. After the incident of 1645 the ferry from Black Rock was closed down by Cromwell, but later, after a lawsuit between Thomas Lewis, of St. Pierre, who owned the new passage, and the Duke of Beaufort, who owned the Beachley-Aust ferry, the Lewises continued the service.

Long before the railways began, steam packets were introduced on the new passage. These ran from 1826 until the opening of the Severn Tunnel in 1886. A short branch line was laid from Portskewett to Black Rock in 1850; this must have been a great convenience to travellers from the ferry, as it has been in later years to Really Important People who have used it as a dormitory line.

The Black Rock Inn at the "new passage" (note the spy-glass in the porch).

At the Black Rock Hotel, Mrs. Lee was kindness personified. She showed me the apartments which had once been the bar and the smoking rooms; she pointed to the window-seats, with their views over the Severn and she indicated the extent of the damage done in the disasterous fire of 1948.

I asked her if there was any special purpose in the upright elliptical windows in both walls of the porch. She took me up into the bar and placed me in line with the two windows. Immediately (for the windows were lenses) I had an enlarged view of the estuary, with the New Passage Hotel across the water.

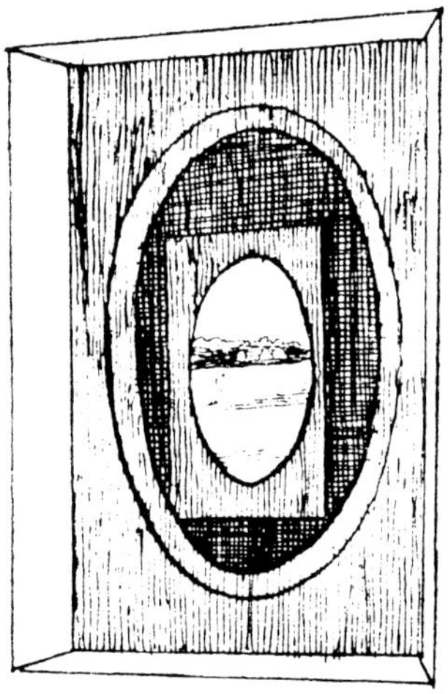

The vertical elliptical lenses in the porch of Black Rock Inn.

Standing at Mrs. Lee's front door I could imaging the scene as the stage-coach came down the road in mid-winter and the shivering passengers rushed into the inn for warmth and refreshment before facing the rigours of the crossing to Gloucestershire.

Return to the previous road junction. (Near here can be seen Heston Brake tumulus.) Turn right and continue to join the A48. Turn right with care and after passing St. Pierre Golf Course, turn right for Mathern.

The road from Black Rock inland meets the main road at Pike House. Opposite is a gate, strung with barbed wire and with a mass of undergrowth beyond. Through that gateway I (as did my neolithic ancestors before me) used to make my way to Heston Brake tumulus. If you would like to feel cold shivers down your spine, choose a moonlit midnight next summer and visit this long barrow alone.

Heston Brake Tumulus by Moonlight.

It is crowned by a rectangle of recumbent stones, terminating at the east end in what might have been a late stone age portrayal of a knife and chopping block and beneath is the communal burial chamber, about 26ft. by 5ft.

Here, in 1888, excavators found human bones, relics of perhaps 2,000 B.C. and in the soil of the cairn, some pottery of later ages. Garn Llwyd, Gwern-y-Cleppa and Heston Brake are our three outstanding dolmens.

At **Mathern** I remembered the magical legend of Tewdrig — the martyr king. Weary of the cares of monarchy, he had handed the crown to his son Meurig (whose name is commemorated in Pwllmeyric) and retired to Tintern, there to seek peace in solitude. But Tewdrig was not destined to die a recluse. When the Saxons attacked his realm the young King Méurig sent in desperation to his father, who once again led his troops into battle, some say at Tintern, others at Bath. The old warrior won a notable victory, but also suffered a mortal wound.

He was drawn from the battlefield by two yoked stags. Wherever they halted, fountains gushed forth and as they approached the Severn the wagon was broken, a very clear stream gushed forth and there Tewdrig died.

His son built a mud and wattle chapel near and later, a stone church was erected on the site. This,

The Church of St. Tewdric, Mathern.

or perhaps a later building, was incorporated in the present Mathern Church and, as the wall-tablet describes, the body of the martyr-king was buried before the altar.

In 1614, Bishop Francis Godwin had the royal tomb reopened and found alongside the stone coffin containing the bones of the king, an urn which held the heart of Miles Salley, Bishop of Llandaff, who had directed that while his body was to be interred at Bristol, his heart was to lie before the altar at Mathern.

An old lady who had lived at Mathern wrote in 1946 to tell me of one of her vivid memories. When she was very young — actually it was in 1881 — the vicar had taken her into the church and shown her a big hole that had been dug in the chancel. There, in a stone coffin, she saw the remains of King Tewdrig, with the hole made by the spear-point still visible in his skull.

Meurig and his son Brochmael made three grants of land to the Bishops of Llandaff. The southern boundary of their manor extended from St. Pierre Pill to Hunger Pill, near the mouth of the Wye; and inland it extended probably to include Runston. Thus after the Conquest, the Bishops were feudal, lords, tenants-in-chief of the crown.

The figure of Christ in the east window shows his head fallen sideways to the north. I was therefore not suprised to find that the axis of the chancel slewed northwards from the nave axis, giving yet another example of ancient symbolism.

I read again the inscription on the north wall of the chancel: I admired the reredos, with its figures of King Tewdrig, Bishop Marshall, Bishop Morgan and Bishop Hughes: I examined the piscina and the two "squints", and then settled to a close study of the brass on the south wall of the nave. In this study I was helped by a little Mathern boy, who had eyesight as keen as his intelligence and who is proud to possess the names of a great Scottish poet.

Philip and Alice Hughes.

This most interesting brass commemorates Philip and Alice Hughes. Philip, who died in 1562, is bearded and wears a long coat. Alice, who survived him by five years, displays the picturesque hat which I have noted elsewhere in Gwent, reminiscent of the headgear of Breton nuns. Both figures wore the ruffs in vogue during the reign of Elizabeth I.

Cut into the brass is the following verse, which I hope you will be able to read:

"O chrift oure god fuer hope
of healpe befyde ye have we non
Thy truth we love and falfhode
hate be thouee our gyde alone.
In molten metal or carved ftone
no confidence we have, But in
thy deathe, and precious blood or fowels fro hell to fave."

Before leaving the churchyard, I took another glance at the tower. Bishop Marshall's coats of arms and the very long sundial arm casting its shadow on to figures which must have been painted so large for sailors on the Severn to see.

All this is but a portion of the treasures of Mathern Church. But where is the well where the water gushed forth? Returning from Mathern, I halted at the end of the stone wall of Mathern House and found the well. The water no longer gushes, but is covered with weed.

In the 19th Century Nennius wrote of a great wonder in the region of Gwent — the spring in the valley of Meurig's Well. When men washed their hands there they stood on a log of wood. At spring tide the sea overflowed the land and drew the log back with it. For three days the log was tossed on the ocean, but on the fourth it was back at the blessed Tewdig's Spring. To test the truth of this story, one of the villagers buried the log in the earth at the next spring tide, but on the fourth day it was found at the spring. And before the end of that month the rustic was dead.

Return to the A48, turn left and return towards Newport via Crick, Caerwent, Penhow and Llanbedr. Then turn left along the B4245 for Llanmartin.

A view of St. Martin's church, Llanmartin.

Four churches in Monmouthshire were dedicated to St. Martin — at Pen-y-Clawdd, Cymyoy, Trewyn (traditional) and **Llanmartin**. I find pleasure in the thought of the Welsh worshippers paying a compliment to their visitors from Gaul and Brittany by dedicating their little sanctuaries to the saintly 4th century Bishop of Tours. Let us remember that Armistice day, November 11, is also Martinmass.

So Llanmartin has seen perhaps a milleium. In a field south-east of the church an object was found which had seen many millenia. It was an Old Stone Age hand-axe which fitted my hand perfectly and actually had an indentation for my thumb.

As we stood in the vestry doorway the rector indicated the foundations of the Morgan chapel, so inexplicably destroyed, with all its treasures except one, in 1858. The surviving memorial to Sir Thomas Morgan, the first knight of Pencoed and his family, stands in the north of the chancel, under an altar slab still displaying five "wound" crosses.

Of the Morgan family memorial I wrote in 1954: "The central panel shows an angel supporting a shield of arms the impalement of which have bared knees, the first also bearing his breast, maybe to display a chain and jewel, while the fourth also bares his breast and all, except the first, are hooded. The sixth figure, front view, is kneeling sideways.

"The five female figures nearest the centre wear similar and becoming hats, three of them display beads, the next a rose-shaped ornament and the next a pendant jewel. "Notice, however, that the two figures on the left have neither headwear nor ornament and bear in mind that Sir Thomas Morgan had but five daughters. He had also eight sons, seven shown."

The Morgan family memorial.

This is no stylised family group. Every face is careful, individual portraiture — a tribute to the sculptor of C 1510, when Sir Thomas died.

My illustration is from a drawing I made in 1954, but long before, in 1923, I had written of these people of Pencoed, "Doleful, melancholy kneels cheek by jowl with half-restrained hillarity; shyness next to the sophistication of a Hollywood star".

Bishton is of course bishops' town, but if you are Welsh you prefer the splendid and sonorous name Llangadwaladr. The church, founded about 570 A.D., is dedicated to Cadwaladr the Blessed, a saint of that time.

In *The Book of Llandaff* we read that Gwaednerth killed his brother Merchion and was therefore excommunicated for three years. On the accession of a new bishop he was pardoned and gave to God and Llandaff all the land, the woods and the sea coast of Llan Cadwaladr. This makes it clear that the "Llan" extended in those days down to the Roman sea wall and included all the "Rotten Lands".

Earthworks near Castle farm, Bishton, mark the site of "Lanckiscastle" which must be Llangadwaladr Castle, where the bishops of Llandaff lived at times. It was here in 1361, that John Pascall, bishop, fled when the plague was raging at Cardiff. He fled in vain, for he died of the plague at Bishton.

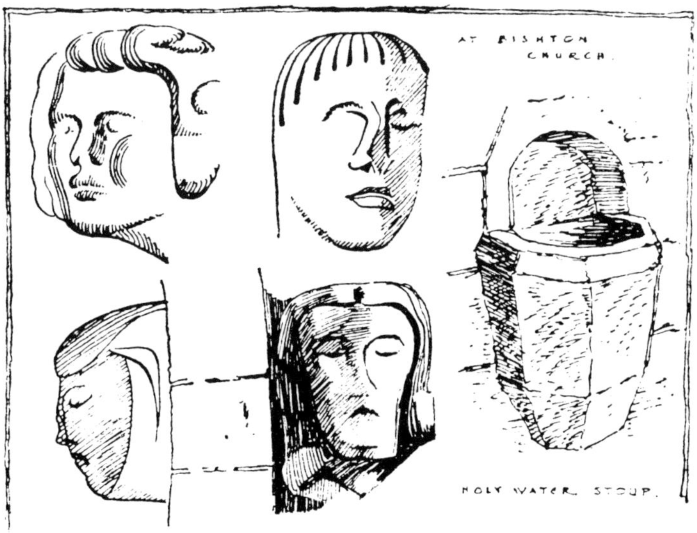

Sculptural heads at Bishton Church.

Bishton Church.

The church has a north porch only. I am sure that originally the entrance was from the main road through a south porch, but when the church (except the tower) was rebuilt in 1887, old traditions were flouted and a northern entrance was made. At the same time the unusually large holy water stoup was taken from the south to the north entrance.

When the four scultpured heads were inserted in the chancel arch I cannot guess. Known as "the priest, the monk, the nun and the happy man", they have the same individual treatment as the heads to be seen at Magor and may be by the same sculptor. There are excellent heads also on the tower.

Leaving the church, I saw the village farm of the Tamplins, the village pound and away behind the chapel alongside the hollow way to the castle, an ancient house named Heol Andrew. Here I met Mr. Rawlings.

Now Mr. Rawlings is a church-warden. As such his word cannot be challenged. Sitting in the kitchen of his early seventeenth century house I asked him to tell me about the highwayman.

"It was my mother who told me," he averred. "At Castle farm one night long years ago Mr. Waters, the farmer, did not return from Newport. His horse came home with one jack-boot in the stirrup; and by Longditch Wood, they found him with his pockets emptied by a highwayman."

"That's not all," continued Mr. Rawlings. "When I was in my late teens I was leaning on a gate on the same hill with two other young men: it was late evening. Suddenly something awful passed me and went into the wood. I looked at my pals; they looked at me, then we made quick for home, for we had all seen the same thing — a cloaked figure with no head!"

In Llanmartin turn right and follow the road to Bishton where the church will be found on the west side of the village on the road to Llanwern.

At Llanwern, St. Mary's welcomes the newcomers.

The oldest map of Monmouthshire, now in the Bodleian library at Oxford, shows two "roads" only. One is the great ridge way through Wentwood to Christchurch, over the ford where Newport bridge now stands and so westwards; the other crosses the sea moors from the landing camp at Sudbrook, joining the ridge way at Christchurch. Alongside this latter road stand the churches of Bishton and St. Mary's Llanwern.

It is possible to recognise very early camps, settlements and enclosures ("llans") by their circular or elliptical shape. In Gwent there are a number of circular churchyards alongside ancient tracks — e.g. Gwernesney, Wolvesnewton, Kilgwrrwg — and to these must be added **Llanwern**.

"Llanwern" is the enclosure of the alders, or marsh. The mighty buttresses at each corner of the church tower and at the east end indicate the unstable nature of the ground, even though the churchyard is above the marsh.

Like Itton and Sudbrook, Llanwern church appears to have been designed as a private chapel, its simple interior consisting only of nave and tower-room, separated by a narrow, tall early English arch. In the south-east corner is a piscina of unusual beauty, while the windows contain glass painted in the 1850's by Miss Salusbury.

Why, I am asked do butterflies appear on some of the monuments and tombstones in St. Mary's? The shield of arms of the Vans bore a chevron between three butterflies. A good example may be seen on the tombstone (which has been moved from the east to the west of the church floor) of "*Lewis Vanne, Esq., of Coldra House and Llanwern, and Sheriff of Monmouthshire in 1634, who married Cicely, daughter of Sir Rowland Williams, of Llangibby Castle and is burred in Christchurch.*"

From Llanwern Church continue to reach the village. Turn right and then go on to join the A455. Turn right for the Coldra junction.

EDITOR'S NOTES

The Caldicot Levels is an area of fascinating history with a strange unique atmosphere, that in recent years has been considerably under threat from industrial development and proposals for an airport, a Severn barrage scheme and a nuclear power station.

St. Mary's church, Nash, with its graceful spire has an exterior that is in strange contrast to the ugly interior mentioned by Fred, but next door more appealing to some, can be found the Waterloo Inn.

At Goldcliff the ancient method of fishing with putchers laid on trestle racks still continues, but now conical baskets are not of withy but made of aluminium wire. A coastal footpath now starts at Goldcliff providing a waymarked route to Mathern.

Redwick now has an additional item of curiosity for a local craftsman Hubert Jones has constructed a stone bus shelter. It contains a cider press and many fascinating old stones. Nearby is a set of ancient looking stocks which he also made.

Undy has been much developed in recent years and the small village is now surrounded by a large housing estate and the same fate has also altered the neighbouring village of Magor.

At Sudbrook the ivy covered ruins of Trinity Chapel are still standing but if they are not given some attention in the near future it will not be long before the chapel is just a heap of stones.

Black Rock now offers a car park and picnic site and it is also a stopping point on the Coastal Walk. The old inn was pulled down over a decade ago but the ferry slipway is still to be seen and from here is a fine view of the Severn Bridge, which itself will in time be rivalled by yet another 'new passage' for a second Severn Bridge is planned.

Mathern with its beautiful palace and noble church is unspoilt but unfortunately the historic well of St. Tewdrig has been 're-constructed' and given the concrete treatment.

Bishton and Llanwern are now of course both dominated by the sight, smell and sounds of the giant Llanwern Steel Works.

A Goldcliff putcher.

CHAPTER NINE

The Lower Wye Valley

St. Arvans — Gaer Hill — Moss Cottage — Tintern — Llandogo — Whitebrook — Trellech — Devauden — Piercefield.

Leaving the A48 follow the A466 past Chepstow Race Course to St. Arvans and bear left in the village along the B4293.

St. Arvans church.

The neat village of **St. Arvans** has always been for me a halfway spot for Trellech or Tintern. Following a kind invitation from Colonel R. Roderick Hill I made a closer investigation of the village and its setting and found it full of interest.

The village chuirch must be one of the few with dormer windows. Maybe the architect who planned the rebuilding in 1884 was also a poet, and inserted these bedroom lights for the saints sleeping below. The tower, which had been previously square, was remodelled into an octagonal shape with four long and four short sides. It contains the bell of 1751 inscribed. "Prosperity to this parish."

Of particular interest is the south doorway into the chancel, which is Norman. A big stone lintel of unusual shape rests on two Norman capitals, one decorated the other plan, and is surmounted by a semi-circular archway, but the tympanum space is now filled with masonry.

A pleasing light from upper and lower windows fills the interior. Pleasing also is the pride of their church displayed by the parishoners. For the whole building and its contents, as we used to say, are as bright as a new pin. Yet two objects of great antiquity are preserved.

In the east window of the south aisle is a sepulchral effigy, the head and feet of which have disappeared, but the hands, foled in prayer, and the robe, may be of a priest. The east window of the aisle contains a slab, which in the opinion of Dr. Nash Williams, dates from the tenth century. It is "a Latin wheel-cross of Celtic type, flanked by panels containing bird-headed angels, and in its likeness to cross-slabs of Scotland and the Isle of Man illustrates the close artistic relationship which existed among the different parts of the ancient Celtic church of Britain."

Hedge decorations at St. Arvans.

I drove from St. Arvans and climbed the hill past the unique topiary exhibitions. These trimmed and clipped lonicera bushes make convincing studies of yachts and tugs, dogs and ducks, rabbits and peacocks, while in the background is a monumental portrayal of the Queen Mary. Each sculpture, if I may use that term, satisfies inspection from every angle and I recommend my readers to climb St. Arvans hill and enjoy Mr. Pritchard's art.

Soon I took the pleasant field-road on the right to Gaer Hill Farm. Here I met Mr. Miles, a man of Kent, and Mrs. Miles, a woman of Gwent (Llangwm), both proud of their origins, and equally proud of their hilltop home.

We spent some time examining the view. "When the Queen was due to cross the ferry last month," said Mrs. Miles, "we decorated our house with every available flag, and then, through powerful fieldglasses, were able to see every incident of the embarkation and crossing. We like to think that Her Majesty looked up and saw our welcome to her."

Haze over the distance robbed me of the view of Bath Abbey, but we had the bird's eye prospect of the meeting of Wye and Severn, of the Denny, of Howick, Itton, Grey Hill, the racecourse, and the park which is south-east Gwent.

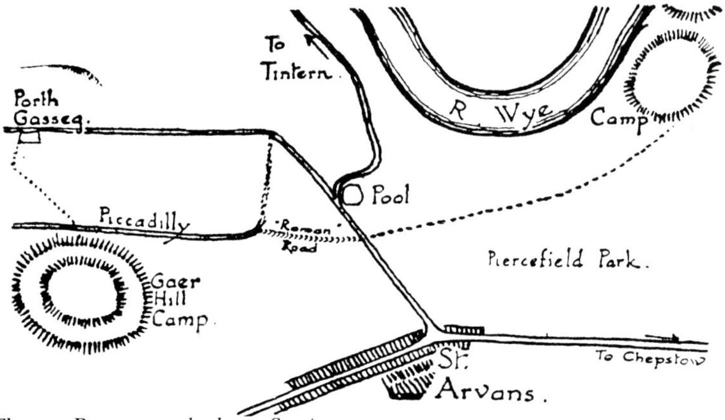

The pre-Roman track above St. Arvans a century ago. (Not to scale).

Mr. Miles and I spent an exhilarating hour touring the camp and his 155-acre farm. At 850 feet above sea level, and measuring 300 yards by 200 yards, this oval hilltop fort retains part of its outer embankment, with an entrance from "Piccadilly" on the east. The inner defence and the outer western embankment have been ploughed out. Mr. Miles showed me a central hollow, which has for some years increased in depth: here as elsewhere, he has "divined" the presence of water.

At this height I should have expected to find the land given over to grazing.. We walked through a big cornfield, where the wheat, sown in March, has grown knee-high in this dry summer, and promises a bountiful harvest.

From the top the view was of the Wyndcliff, Porthgasseg, Tidenham Chase and the Wye Valley (Tintern hidden in a fold in the hills), Brockweir, Trellech beacon, the Skirrid and Sugar Loaf.

Return to the A466 and drive on towards Tintern to reach a car park below the Wyndcliff where a waymarked trail may be followed up the 365 steps to the viewpoint on top of the Wyndcliff.

The **Wyndcliff** has been an autumn destination for many years. It is associated in my mind with so many delightful people, so many gorgeous mornings and evenings, that the news of the impending demolition of Moss Cottage caused my heart a pang in place of a beat.

Moss Cottage, Wyndcliff, Tintern, 1957 (now demolished).

Mr. Clark had written to me: "Moss Cottage, now derelict, is to come down, and the forestry people feel that you may wish to record it while you can."

A primrose bloomed on the bank as I stood surveying the cottage. Melancholy as it was on that cold grey day, to contrast the ruined fragment with the bright, pretty, busy little thatched retreat through which we had been so often admitted to the enchantment of the great cliff.

In *About Chepstow* Ivor Waters tells us that the Duke of Beaufort built Moss Cottage under the Wyndcliff as a picturesque feature and placed inside it a table made from a slab of a walnut tree which grew in the ditch of Chepstow castle. The cottage was well known by 1830, for in the *Guide to Town and Neighbourhood of Chepstow*, printed by J. Clark in that year we have an account written in the curvaceous high-heeled prose of those days.

"The rooms in this habitation are neatly laid out after the manner of Indian wigwams: every part is thickly lined with moss and the pleasing view from the gothic windows renders it a cool and tranquil

half-hour's retreat. This cottage by the liberality of the Duke of Beaufort is appropriated to the gratuitous accommodation of the picnic parties and other visitors frequenting these romantic scenes. It is recommended that parties do bring refreshments with them. Water, milk, etc., for tea can be procured of the person who resides at the cottage."

The Wye in these parts has tempted many an author to burst into song. Wordsworth spread his wings in glorious efforts to pinion the valley-beauty. Lesser writers spread thick sweet jam over their pages in polysyllabic rapture, but I recall the silence of my friends when they took the view from the Wyndcliff of Llancaut and Piercefield, Wye and Severn, Gloucestershire and Somerset, aye and beyond to the Holms and Penarth Head.

Many of the visitors to Wyndcliff a century ago took pistols in order to count the echoes. Heath reported that there were usually five repetitions of the explosion distinctly heard "from rock to rock": often seven; and if the weather was calm, nine echoes.

Tidenham cliffs were a line of light in the sombre landscape; sombre too were the woodlands which unfolded us as we dropped gently into **Tintern**.

Strange, we said, to revel in golden glory in November, and to meet winter's sleep in April, a sound sleep under the brown beech blankets! Enough to send the swifts and swallows back to Ghana!

Tintern October-end 1961.

Bright sunshine, however, picked out the stonework on the Abbey, and turned a couple of brave willow into golden fountains. Long years ago we used to see Tintern each year under the harvest moon. While the crowds surged into the Abbey we awaited the moon rise from our hillside churchyard (St. Mary's on the Hill). From my own record made in 1930 I extract a few impressions:

"From the black hill opposite came a quivering sound, rich and deep, like the voice of Paul Robeson. Louder and clearer it grew, and suddenly across the velvet shadows was drawn a string of gems, moving to the sound of the deep bass note. The sight and sound ceased. Silence and

Tintern Abbey   19th C. engraving.

View from the Wyndcliff.

The Moon and Sixpence, Tintern.

darkness once more descended." (That was the train on the Wye Valley line which, because it was uneconomic was eliminated.)

"Above the hill, however, the sky changed. As we watched, the summit of the hill darkened. A mist of faint light arose from the valley. Brighter the sky glowed, more clearly the edge of the black hill was etched, and slowly, with infinite grace and grandeur, came forth the moon. As she raised herself from beyond the hilltop a faint wind stirred, and the small leaves ofthe churchyard tree flickered, black as the hill-top across the silver wonder. "We peered into the grey valley. Tenderly the light bent downwards, painting the upper edge of every Abbey detail. In two minutes, grey against grey, exquisite, mystical. St. Mary's of the Valley stood revealed."

St. Mary's on the Hill, Tintern.

Yes, the Abbey church like the church on the hill, was dedicated to St. Mary. To many of us the upper church has been merely a point of vantage for viewing the abbey, but the little sanctuary has its own points of interest.

The saddle-backed tower-cum-entrance is near the western end of the north wall. The external doorway is topped by a single, chamfered lintel-stone, and the quoins of the tower are in excellent presentation. Ironwork on the door, with fleur-de-lis terminals, is similarly well-preserved in spite of the altitude.

Trefoiled window arches everywhere may be a symbol of the Trinity and the same decoration is repeated within. Close to the entrance and in the thickness of the wall, I saw a remarkable recess, possibly for an image. The mouldings, triple-membered, and the three steps leading up to the little platform are impressive.

Good workmanship also is seen in the double piscina set in the south walls of the chancel. In the north wall is fixed a stone bracket with delicate ornamentation. These three items suggest that masons from the Abbey may have helped to beautify the little upland church. Unusual, too is the simple font on its long column:

The woodwork in the roof is unceiled and comprises some massive items. Pleasant it is to read that the screen, pulpit and sanctuary chair, were made by William Jones, who had been the parish clerk for more than forty years.

Of the monumental masonry in St. Mary's churchyard I need but record my astonishment that it was possible to haul and install such massive and baroque memorials on such a site.

On now through the village, under Barbadoes wood, we make for Tintern Parva, pass St. Michael's church and the superannuated railway station, the Brockweir view, then Coed Beddick, Coed Ithel (where once was an ironstone furnace) Bargain wood, and Llandogo.

The wireworkers' cottages, Tintern.

Iron-works at Tintern? Smoke belching over the sacred abbey ruins and up the romantic **Angidy Valley?** In truth yes, for when the Hon. John Byng was touring the Wye Valley in the late 18th century he recorded the view of flames from the furnaces opposite his bedroom window in the Beaufort hotel.

It is quite possible that iron was produced at Tintern from the earliest days. Plentiful supplies of ore were available from the Forest of Dean, and Tintern was well-placed for producing the crude iron needed for the Roman forges at Ariconium and Worcester, and the "college of armourers" at Bath. And even before the Romans came most of the tools used in husbandry or handicraft (except screws and scissors) were in vogue, and made of iron.

In additon to the iron ore, vast quantities of charcoal were required. The furnaces which Byng saw at Tintern were fuelled by coal (from Lancashire!), but before the days of coal the wise ironmaster bought all the woodlands within a wide radius of his works, for it took 16 sacks of charcoal — one sack holding 12 bushels — to produce one ton of pig iron. Many square miles of open country were forests before the iron age.

Yet we are not sure of any forges in Tintern in Roman days, or yet in Norman times, when there were four such forges in Monmouth. There are persistent legends of iron-works run by the monks of Tintern, but I have been unable to discover that they used the waters of the Angidy and Wye for anything but "grist and tucking mills," and to carry off the abbey drainage.

The Angidy Valley may be reached by turning left behind the George Hotel in Tintern and following the road towards Trellech Grange.

In the spacious days of the first Elizabeth, when men's minds were roving outwards, skilled metal workers were encouraged to explore for and "manure" (manufacture) metals of all kinds. Among them were William Humfrey (assay-master to the mint) and Christopher Schutz from

Saxony, Schutz had devised a method of "mollifying and manuring" iron by the right use of calamine stone (zic ore), and the "drawing and forging the same into wire and plates."

Recognising the importance of this method, the "Society for the Minerals and Battery Works" was informed, including many of the great figures of Elizabeth's days. Humfrey and Schutz were sent to seek a suitable spot for the site of the proposed works. The Earl of Pembroke (one of the directors of the society); wished them to set up the factory in the grounds of Bristol Castle, but the water-power there was inadequate so they inspected all *"the pleasant rivers on Severn-side,"* but found them all busily turning flour and cloth mills. So they crossed the Severn and found an ideal spot at Tintern.

Here the *"house for wire"* was built, and further houses (still standing, and my sketch shows) erected for the German workmen who had accompanied Schutz. Soon Tintern came to be known as the site for thc manufacture of wire, which was to be used chiefly for making carding-combs for clothiers.

Now Hunfrey and Schutz were dependent for the quality of their wire upon a supply of "Osmond" iron. Unable to obtain it, they lost £500 in their first year of production. A new and skilful wire-drawer, Barnes Keyser, altered the machinery and tried to instruct the workers in new methods, but found them "soe dulle learners," and in the second year a loss of £800 was sustained, aggravated by the defalcation of their clerk, one Crump, who "ymbesiled" from them £300.

The ore from which this iron was reduced was a brown hematite rich in phosphorous, dredged from the bottom of rivers and lakes in northern Europe, and Hanbury owned "2 or 3 iron works in Wales, whereat he made much merchant iron to greate gayne." (One of these works was probably Pontypool, on the site of the charcoal furnace and forges.)

An examination of the works revealed low stocks, gross mis-management and heavy debts. Management was undertaken by Richard Hanbury and Sir Richard Martyn, and with plentiful supplies of Osmond iron all went well, and Tintern wire became famous.

By good fortune I met Mr. Edgar Waite, whose father and grandfather were wire drawers in the Tintern mills. I asked him if he could still locate the sites of the mills in the Angidy valley.

"One mill," he recalled, "was at Crown cottage, another at the bungalow owned by Mr. Jones, the baker, and the Chapel Mill was higher up the valley near the chapel, which is now Chapel garage." Chapel garage is the central building in my sketch. The Angidy Brook flows just behind the building.

Continue through Tintern (perhaps stopping at the Old Station on the way for a brief pause and refreshments) and then on to Llandogo.

To Odoceous, Bishop of Llandaff in the Sixth Century, we owe the strange name of one of the exquisite Wye Valley hamlets — **"Llandogo."** The saintly Bishop had his dwelling and served his God on the banks of the mountain stream which cascades in fantastic leaps from the moorland down the steep hillside to the village.

Einion, king of Glewyssig, and his huntsmen had followed a stag for many hours through the wild woods. The hounds were about to leap on the stag when the weary beast dragged its body on to the cloak of Odoceous and collapsed, whereupon nothing would induce the hounds to attack it.

When the King discovered that the cloak belonged to the Bishop he prayed for pardon, bestowed the stag on Odoceous, and presented to Llandaff the whole of the ground over which he had hunted that day from the Red Pool to the Wye.

We recognise the Red Pool as the Virtuous Well of Trellech, but we know not where the Bishop dwelt, and the ancient church of Llandogo was demolished and rebuilt in the bleak middle years of the last century.

The culverted brook disappears under the main road and the Sloop Inn.

On a sunny November afternoon we halted at **The Sloop Inn** at Llandogo, and walked around the old house. The original entrance and frontage were towards the river and on this wall we found the inscription:

This reminded us that the patrons of The Sloop must have arrived by water, as no roads were laid in the valley until the early years of the nineteenth century. The name of the inn recalled the busy days when at the head of the tide. Llandogo was the terminus of a busy trade route to Bristol. So famous were the Llandogo trows (or sloops) that one of Bristol's grand old inns, the Llandoger Trow (where Long John Silver served before setting out for "Treasure Island") was named after such a craft, and a trow appears on the seal of the Borough of Monmouth.

Barges from Monmouth, Ross and even Hereford, brought their goods to the wharves at Llandogo and Brockweir, and many a tale is told of the feuds between the barge-owners on the one hand, and the salmon fishers and millers on the other, who found that the construction of weirs was a quick road to fortune.

The Sloop inn, we noticed with surprise, was built over the swiftly-flowing brook. "Can this water have come down from the waterfall?" asked Robert. And when I assured him, he commanded with seven-year-old impudence, that we should discover the waterfall. We took the good winding road up the hill — two miles long — in short stages. Ever and anon, through and over the honey-hued larch forest, we stopped to take the views. They were incredibly beautiful in the November sunshine — those trees, rocks, cottages and the blue river. But where was the waterfall?

Suddenly and shrilly, Robert (who has not read "Westerns" for nought) shouted: "I can see it shooting out of that gulch!" And against the skyline were **Cleddon Shoots**, cascades of molten silver against the shadowed cliff.

Cleddon Shoots above Llandogo.

On again, up again, until we reached the heath, where the rich russet was relieved by the plantations of conifer. Along one of these plantations some genius had set an edging of crimson buried bushes. We turned right, and right again, past Cleddon Hall, where Bertrand Russell was born, and soon afterwards we pulled up sharp to save ourselves from descending a forest path into Llandogo.

There, on the right, was the first cascade, and we were able to imagine this water leaping and leaping down the brown hillside, darting under The Sloop, and silvering the tawny flood-water of the Wye.

A graceful curve around Cuckoo Wood brought us in view of Bigsweir bridge where everybody crosses into Gloucestershire for the run through Redbrook to Monmouth. We ignored the bridge and drove past Pilstone parallel to the river until a bend to the left led us into the valley of Gwenffrwd — the Whitebrook.

New Mill, Whitebrook.

Industry has ravaged so many Monmouthshire valleys that it is refreshing to find, as in **Whitebrook valley**, that man's work has at times increased the natural beauty. At two or three points the white rushing stream — for that is "gwen-ffrwd" — has been dammed into exquisite fish and mill ponds and traces of the famous Whitebrook paper mills, including a handsome down-draught shaft of stone, are themselves picturesque elements in the landscape.

Whitebrook millstones, known as Welsh stones, were made in the district from the "pudding stones" which abound, but this unlike the paper making and flour milling, has left scarcely any remains.

Climb up through the Whitebrook Valley to reach the ridge road (B4293) and turn left for Trellech.

Trellech from the Tintern Road.

Thirteen centuries ago King Ffernwael gave the church of "Trylec" to Llandaff, but nothing remains of that church or of the first Norman church. **Trellech church** as we know it is Early English, of the thirteenth and fourteenth centuries, and belonged to the priory at Chepstow.

On the inner side of the south door you will discern the date 1595 and the sacred letters IHS. Within all is light and aspiring, the tall arch at the west leading to the tower with its three ancient bells, and the coat of arms of Charles II dated 16CR83.

Imposing arcades separate nave from aisles and these are surmounted by the fifteenth century clerestory, which adds much light. In the south aisle see the sandstone piscina with its unusual trefoli design and small pedestal.

You will see that the pulpit, once a "three-decker," is dated 1640 and a portion of oak panelling 1639, but you will regret with me that the latter is completed with an addition of pitch-pine. Of course good solid oak, however, are the sanctuary rails and the carved chairs. The church plate is of the sixteenth and seventeenth centuries.

Now study the most remarkable sundial in this island. It used to stand, so Mr Ellaway the village carpenter instructs me, in the field north of the church where is now the school path, and rested not on its present base which is modern, but on a larve inverted stone bowl, which, as you will see (for it is close at hand) is the original font. The field was known as the "Clock-house Field," referring to the sundial.

The dial itself has on each of its four sides a Latin word, the sentence reading:

HORA DIEM DEPASCIT EUNDO
(the hour passing consumes the day).

The hours are marked, surprisingly, on all the sides. It rests on a remarkable stone pedestal on three sides of which are panels with representations of the show-places in the village.

The southern panel shows the Terret Tump, surmounted by the words Magna Mole (great because of its tump) and below O QUOT HOC SEPULTI (O how many are buried here!)

The old sun dial in Trellech Church.

On the eastern panel are the three stones marked 8, 10, 14 (feet high) with the inscriptions MAIOR SAXIS (greater because of its stones) and HIC FUIT VICTOR HARALDUS (here Harold was victorious).

The northern panel shows the virtuous well with MAXMA FONTE (Greatest because of its Well) and DOM MAGD PROBERT OSTENDIT (Lady Magdalene Probert(?) throws it open).

The last translation is doubtful, but as Lady Probert was the widow of the High Sheriff and Member of Parliament (Sir George Probert of Pantglas) it may be that she helped in its preservation. The date of the sundial is 1689,, there is nothing on the western panel, and the base of the monument is modern.

The sundial at Trellech announces that the village is great by reason of its tump, greater because of its three stones, but greatest because of its virtuous well. Yet my prosaic son Robert mistook the well for an air raid shelter!

At Llandogo I described how King Einion presented to Llandaff the ground on which he had hunted, "from the red pool to the Wye." The Red pool was on the site of the virtuous well, the chalybeate waters of which are certainly red, and certainly possessed of a hideously medicinal taste.

The steam which fills the well bubbles forth just near the barn on the Beacon slopes. It flows past Trellech, through Woolpitch Wood, down to Penarth Mill, and so far has been known as Penarth Brook. Soon afterwards it becomes the Olway.

The well is a basin in an arched recess of a stone wall which forms the rear of a semi-circular chamber of masonry sunk into a meadow. Steps leading down-wards, a stone seat, and two recesses for votive offerings, tell of pilgrimages throughout the centuries, but the view of the lovely village may have had a more virtuous effect on the pilgrims than had the bitter waters.

This stone structure, erected possibly by one of the Rumseys, is worthy of careful preservation. Will the boys of Trellech take charge of it, remove the weeds and report any part which needs attention?

The virtuous well at Trellech.

The Three Stones at Trellech.

Like many others in our land the virtuous well has its own legend. Any lass who wished to learn how long she would need to wait for her wedding day would drop a pebble into the well and count one month for every bubble.

From Mr. Reynolds, of Trellech, I collected the classic legend of the witch of Pont-y-Saeson. Trellech Moor was once a vast park, as is shown in the grant by Gilbert Marshall, Earl of Pembroke to the abbot and monks of Tintern "for the refection of the infirm brothers abiding in the same house they do have both shoulders of all wild animals of the wood, to wit stag and hind, deer and roe taken in our park of Trellech." This, by the way explains the place-name "Park House." Such wild animals have long since disappeared and the sportsmen have concentrated on coursing the hare.

"long years ago," said Mr. Reynolds, "there was a hare on the moor which they could not catch. With hounds on his heels he would bound across the moor, swing left down the Tintern valley, and then, just as he was nearing the witch's cottage at Pont-y-Saeson, disappear into thin air."

At last our fellows decided to borrow a prize greyhound bitch from up the valleys. When all was ready they put her on the scent and soon hare and hound were leaping, leaping! Down the valley shot the hare, but this time, just as he was about to vanish, the bitch nipped him on the rear leg.

The witch wasn't seen for three weeks, when she appeared it was noticed that she was limping and wore a bandage around her left ankle."

From Trellech continue along the B4293 via Cobbler's Plain with extensive views on either side to reach Devauden.

Devauden Church.

In 1739, John Wesley stopped *"on the little green"* of **Devauden** on his way from Chepstow to Usk. *"At 4 p.m.,"* he writes, *"I preached to three or four hundred plain people on 'Christ, our wisdom, righteousness, sanctification and redemption. 'After the sermon, one who I trust is an old disciple of Christ received us into his house; wheither many following I showed them again their need of a Saviour."*

Outside the house, adjoining the Masons' Arms at Devauden Green, I was shown the well-worn mounting block used by John Wesley, but I could not find whose portrait rests high on the wall above.

In addition to John Wesley, Devauden folk remember with honour and affection their saintly old schoolmaster, James Davies who had been appointed as the master of the newly established school at Usk. But in his journeys throughout the countryside the wretchedness of the people weighed on his heart, and the worst conditions of squalor and poverty, of ignorance untold, he found at Devauden.

The parish church was Newchurch, and services, supposed to be fortnightly, were usually held once in six weeks. Some of the people went down the steep hill to Kilgwrrwg, where the rain poured through the roof and where sheep were folded at night.

Then in 1811 the Rev. William Jones was appointed curate of Kilgwrrwg and in 1813 curate of Newchurch. James Davies found in William Jones a twin soul, and between them they planned to save Devauden. Despite difficulties which would have disheartened lesser men, these two decided to build a school. The Duke of Beaufort provided the land; the school, built for 120 children, was opened in 1815, and James Davies, who had been receiving regularly at Usk a salary of £30, resigned his post there and took over the new school at Devauden at a salary which was sometimes less than £15 and never more than £20 a year.

The story of his life at Devauden is a modern version of the life of St. Francis. His school, which was also his home (for he ate and sleep and taught in the same big room) became the centre of help for the whole district. He fed the starving, he clothed and helped the needy; frequently in the bitter winter nights — and it can be bitter at Devauden — it was Davies's blankets which saved the sick and aged from pneumonia while the saintly schoolmaster covered himself with his thin overcoat.

In that room he taught eighty to 100 children. The day was opened and closed with prayer and on Sundays all the children attended his Sunday-school, yet in spite of all his efforts and prayers, "evil still reigned at Devauden," and while his friend William Jones was infusing new life into Newchurch and Kilgwrrwg, Davies knew in his heart that he was called to provide a church at Devauden.

First he had the schoolroom licensed for divine worship in 1829. After it had been ceiled, whitewashed and painted, a pulpit, reading desk and benches were installed, the whole costing James Davies £45 — over twice his annual salary! Here the vicar of Newchurch preached on Sunday evenings.

Next a new schoolroom was built that the consecrated room might be used only for services. Finally, in 1838, the church was consecrated by the Bishop of Llandaff, and James Davies aged 73, had achieved his heart's desire. For seven further years Devauden remained as his Assisi — for never was a saintly man vowed more fervently to poverty — and then at eighty, he took yet another decision.

At Llangattock Lingoed, where he had known his only schooling, he found *"peculiar destitution."* Devauden had now its church and school, but at Llangattock there was no resident priest, and no school.

In 1848, James Davies, aged 83, laid the foundation stone of the new school and for two more years he laboured there unpaid, *"planting an orchard for those who should follow."* Then, beloved by the whole countryside, he died and was buried within sound of his dear children's voices.

I visited **Devauden church**. In imagination I removed the church furniture and replaced the school benches and the old school-master's chairs and table and bed. A hundred ghostly children sat at their lessons. "Jamie" directing them, his saintly ascetic face moved to pleasure at their efforts, his strong hand swift and sure in punishing their misdemeanor.

One young rascal is strapped in the basket and hauled beam-high. The afternoon wears on, the children sing their hymn, say their prayer, and trudge away to their far-flung homes, and the schoolmaster spends the evening visiting the sick.

While dressing on the following morning he hears a yawn from the basket above, and remembers young Lewis of Wolvesnewton has slept all night in the basket!

The basket punishment.

From Devauden continue along the B4293 to St. Arvans and rejoin the A466. If you wish to visit the Pircefield Walks then bear left at Crossway Green and follow the road towards Chepstow. Turn in at the Leisure Centre car park and look out for a sign indicating the Wye Valley Walk which will lead you on a fascinating route above the Pircefield Cliffs and past the viewpoints described by Valentine Morris. See Exploring Gwent by Chris Barber for a more detailed description.

Imagine a river winding like an enormous S, with an upper part bigger than the lower. Fill the upper part with flat meadows, a few white farm buildings and a small ancient church; fill the lower part with woods on high ground, containing one oval and one circular prehistoric encampment. Around the outer curve of the S are stupendous cliffs, partly clothed with verdue and rising at the north to the Wynd Cliff, 771 feet high. You now have some idea of the setting of **Piercefield**.

Piercefield near Chepstow.

The original house, in a park, of 300 acres, was the home of the Walters family. In 1736 it was bought by Colonel Valentine Morris, and it was to his son that the glories of Piercefield were due.

Valentine Morris the younger inherited considerable wealth, married the beautiful and clever Mary Mordaunt, niece of Lord Peterborough, and, as Charles Heath, of Monmouth, quaintly tells us, was "of the first rank of society," living in princely state at Piercefield.

His imagination was fired by the superb beauty of his property. He cleared some eight viewpoints, laid down walks through the forest, along the clifftops, and sometimes down the cliffs; he kept a number of servants whose duties were to show the innumerable visitors around the estate and to see that "collations were indiscriminately offered to them." In addition the name of Valentine Morris became a by-word for benefactions to all in need.

Extravagant living, a weakness for gambling, a run of bad seasons on his West Indian estate, and heavy expenses in a parliamentary election brought about his downfall.

He failed in an attempt to sell Piercefield, and with the whole countryside mourning his departure, he left for St. Vincent's, where he was appointed governor, and by his zeal in promoting the cultivation of the island, won great praise and renewed fortune. Then the French captured the island and he lost all, dying, after a period in a debtor's prison, in 1789.

In 1794 Piercefield was bought by Sir Mark Wood, who rebuilt the mansion, erected the lodges and raised the boundary wall. When Coxe visited Piercefield in 1800 the estate measured 3,000 acres, and the timber alone was valued at £8,000.

The new Piercefield was indeed an imposing edifice, the main building fronted with Ionic pillasters and a semi-circular Doric Portico. At both ends, greenhouses led to Doric wings, respectively a library and a music room. Floors of Dutch oak or black and white marble, inlaid mirrors in mahogany partitions giving far-flung views, walls enriched by fine designs "in relievo," the grand staircase of Painswick stone, and tapestry which once belonged to Louis XVI, combined with the furniture to give an air of taste and splendour. And yet I am told that it was the coldest house in Gwent!

Railings ahead protected us from a fall of 180 feet vertically into the Wye, but there were no railings to interfere with the Lovers' Leap of the legend.

Now we took formation of line ahead, with Michael leading and Caroline acting as whipper-in. The path wound in and out of the steep declevity, the views downwards between the cliff-side trees being of amazing gradeur and the path of sufficient difficulty to demand concentration. Loosened stones disappeared downwards with a velocity I should not have enjoyed.

Suddenly our host announced: "Giant's Cave ahead!" We threaded the cavern and from its depths looked out over the magnificence of cliff and river and distant channel.

"No giant was responsible for this," said the colonel (Colonel Roderick Hill). "It was a Morris production, and to complete the idea he had a Herculean figure hoisted into the cavity above, holding a huge boulder ready to hurl on to the unsuspecting visitor!"

The Giant's Cave, as designed by Valentine Morris.

The descent to the Smugglers' Cave.

The Herculean figure has disappeared, and as the Bookman refused to take his place, we all made our slippery way onwards, until a mark on a rock, recognised by Michael, brought us to a halt.

"This is the way down to the spot where we can view the Smugglers' Cave," announced our guide, but I grieve to record that as I had already slipped once to be grabbed by the Bookman, it was decided that the descent was not for me. So I watched and sketched, while the three intrepid explorers slithered Wye-wards at about sixty degrees.

Valentine Morris had nothing to do with the Smugglers' Cave. Cunningly hidden in the cliff face which holds the rocks known as the Twelve Apostles and Peter's Thumb, it could be reached by water only at high tide. Hauling their booty up the steep cliff must have called for skill and stength on the part of the smugglers.

The return upwards called for fitness on the part of our explorers. I found it engaging to note how ease of breathing varied inversely with the age of the climbers.

Within a few yards now we stumbled on what must have been dubbed the Druids' Temple — a roughly circular distribution of rocks. Near this spot Colonel Hill showed us the path to the ice house which was an outbuilding in which huge blocks of ice were deposited in April, for the purpose of keeping food fresh during the heat of summer.

Leaving the cliff-walk for the open fields, we arrived soon at the ruins of Piercefield House. To our surprise and relief, Caroline, who had disappeared before the descent to the Smugglers' Cave, was standing bside her father's car, which she had driven to meet us.

We stood before the delapidated mansion, replacing in imagination all its magnificence, and unimpressed by the result. Far more thrilling was the view, for although we were only 200 feet above the channel, this elevation emphasised the grandueur of the scene as the lines of the landscape swung gracefully towards the meeting place of Wye and Severn. Placed with an artist's certainty as a lovely focal point, with the sunlight streaming down from behind a high cloud on castle and church and clustered hillside houses, arose Chepstow in all her beauty, and from no other viewpoint have I seen her so exquisite.

The other viewpoints arranged by Valentine Morris were all lost in undergrowth, but Michael made a prolonged attempt to locate the Chinese Seat. In response to repeated shouts, he called back at last. "Can't find it, I'm caught in a bramble bush." I thought of Troy, covered up with weeds, "where Priam's ancient palace stood."

Moonrise at Tintern.

EDITOR'S NOTES

Since Fred Hando departed the Wye Valley has been designated as an Area of Outstanding Natural Beauty which is a development that would most certainly have met with his approval.

On a recent visit to St. Arvans I examined with interest the Tenth Century wheel-cross slab in the church but later failed to see the hedge decorations on the roadside, described by Fred. Nodoubt the hedge artist has also passed on and the new owners have not continued with the work.

Radio masts have now been planted on the summit of Gaer Hill but the view from there is still magnificent and uninterrupted.

Moss Cottage at the foot of the Wyndcliff has long since gone but the 365 Steps have been restored and a circular walk may be followed from a car park, mysteriously up through a gap in the cliffs to reach the Eagle's Nest viewpoint for one of the finest views in Gwent.

Tintern Abbey is still thronged with tourists in summer and I agree with Fred that the best view of the abbey is from the hillside churchyard of St. Mary's. This little church is now a roofless ruin having been abandoned some years ago and mysteriously set on fire during 'some strange goings on' one dark night.

A waymarked path leads across the old railway bridge in Tintern providing a route up through the woods to a viewpoint romantically known as the Devil's Pulpit.

In the Angidy Valley the old iron forge and blast furnace has been excavated, exposed and explained with display panels erected on the site by Gwent County Council. Information about the site may be obtained from the 'Old Station' just to the north of Tintern where the former railway station is now a picnic area with refreshment facilities and a small exhibition telling the story of the Wye Valley line.

The Sloop inn at Llandogo has been much altered over the years and it was awarded the title 'A.A. inn of the year for Wales' in1985.

Trellech has retained its old world charm and its curiosities; the stones, the well, the mound and the sundial continue to attract and intrigue visitors.

In Devauden one may now visit the Beaufort Bird Gardens where exotic birds and rare pheasants may be seen and the beautiful gardens admired.

Walkers following the Wye Valley Walk — a long distance walk starting at Chepstow Castle will pass through the Piercefield woods and several of the named view-points set up by Valentine Morris for sections of the old walks have now been re-opened.

At river level below the woods, the Smugglers' Cave referred to by Fred is now known as Otter Hole. This is now a very extensive cave system which has been opened up by caving enthusiasts. Beneath Chepstow racecourse they have discovered large caverns with magnificent formations but it is a difficult and tiring journey which may only be undertaken by experts. The entrance tothe cave is gated and access controlled to preserve the cave and its formations and keep out inexperienced cavers.

Piercefield mansion is now a very sad ruin. Over the years various plans have been made to rebuild it as a hotel but so far nothing has happened. In many ways it is perhaps better that it should be left as a romantic ruin.

The Royal George, Tintern.

CHAPTER TEN

MEMORIES OF FRED HANDO

Fred Hando was tall with a straight-backed figure. He had a natural charm of manner which helped greatly in gaining entrance to the numerous historical houses where he was always made welcome. Some headmasters I have known could be judged a little stiff and starchy, but not Fred. His sense of humour and impish fun made it a pleasure to be in conversation with him.

During World War 1 he had seen service in the gunners, and when he was young he had been the organist for the chapel in Albert Avenue, Maindee. He had been a teacher and later became the headmaster of Hatherleigh School; a building which he loved and saw that it was well cared for during his period of service there.

His interest in local history was given impetus when he agreed to do some of the sketches for Sir Joseph Bradney's *"History of Monmouthshire."* Later his sketches added greatly to the charm of his weekly Friday night articles in the South Wales Argus. These articles became very popular and given a nice day on the following Sunday you could be certain of seeing a number of his admiring readers following the Friday night's article route.

My contact with him extended over a number of years during which I helped him with local history information and was privileged to accompany him on a number of his journeys in Gwent. As I was Borough Librarian for Newport he referred to me in his article as *"The Bookman."*

His passing meant a great loss to the people who enjoyed his illustrations and articles. It is pleasing to think that he has been remembered by the placing of seats in some of his favourite spots in the county.

W. John Collett

Fred Hando — 'Man of Gwent'.

A letter from an old pupil
"Mr Hando used to give us lessons on the book Treasure Island. He did all the voices in the book — high and low — to make it real for us.

One day he announced to the class that he had a new baby and then Mrs. Hando walked in with a baby in a pram. We all clapped and felt proud. Also one day he came in with a soldier who was an old boy. We talked of war etc.. and Mr. Hando chased one boy down the long corridors of the school with a cane.

Mr. Hando was not averse to speaking to tramps (if the man was an artist). The tramp/artist I knew who was on speaking terms with him was a man called Bill Dixie, now dead. Mr. Hando brought an old man around the classes one day. He was a butler in the school when it was a mansion (private). We all saw him peeping through the window and told the head, who said that he worked in the school in service. Mr. Hando gave him a guided tour to see how different it was. I bet he had a wealth of tales to tell.

Hatherleigh School.

"To be a full-blooded Newport boy it was necessary in my day to have performed several feats. First, of course, came the climbing of Twyn Barllwm; next the climbing of one or more well-known trees; soon followed the test of climbing "straight-legged" the Christchurch hill and swimming in various forbidden waters; and it was a great day when we walked to Cardiff and back."

Cookery class at Hatherleigh.

A Hatherleigh classroom.

We have exams. I ended up 2nd in class. Top marks in arty subjects — bottom in sums etc. We all liked to run into the big bushes; boys used to kiss the girls in same and I buried a tin of coins in the grounds. I wonder if it is still there? Mr. Hando caned 7 or 8 boys one winter for mocking Mr. Hughes — they threw snowballs at Mr. Hughes and Mr. Hando saw them from the Head's window.

I have snaps of the school I took, but none of them indoors. Miss Hall one day caned the whole class of girls. I forget the reason, but it must have been serious. One boy was expelled for an attack on a girl in the air raid shelter.

Good old days. I am now 52 and wish I was there again.

Mr. Hando once said in class — if when you are engaged — to bring your wife to see me a week before the wedding so I can meet you and wish you luck etc. This is a remembrance (strong) I have of him.

Being single I never had the chance to do this.

Also he was a good piano player — so were most of the teachers there. I had the cane once off Mr. Hill and once off Mr. Hando. Mr. Hando caned me for being late. I had a boil on the bottom of my foot but he never believed me.

Good old days — good times to live in. (1946-1950)

I still have my school report for 1946.

R.F. Stevens

A few words from 'Will of the Hills'

Fred Hando was a man of many talents. He was an author whose usage of the English language was delightful and descriptive, able to paint a picture in words — describing so well that a vivid mental picture was evoked.

Of the small mansion of Treowen he wrote — '*...as brown and solid as a Norman keep.*' Other such examples, just as perceptive, are in his books. His artistic ability enabled him to transfer a visual appreciation of a scene to his sketch-pad; such sketches being a delightful feature of his many books on Gwent.

He liked the good things of life, a glass of ale with his friends. Many a proposed journey of exploration was planned in the 'snug' of the Greyhound Inn at Christchurch, discussing the journey to be made with *'the Bookman'*, (John Collet, Borough Librarian) and myself. *'Will of the Hills.'*

I first met Fred about thirty years ago. He had come to the Newport Camera Club meeting to give a talk on the appreciation of a landscape painting and the composition, as a scene contained within the frame of a camera viewfinder.

He suggested that the club members should use their cameras with some definite purposes — to capture the ever-changing scene of the passing years. Also to make a pictorial record of the historic buildings and scenery of Gwent. He spoke with great enthusiasm, leading me to embark on such a project. So in 1965 I was proud and pleased to give him a copy of my illustrated book *West of the Wye — with a camera in Gwent.*

We became firm friends and whenever he went to visit a place or scene of special interest for photographic recording I often accompanied him. My son, Chris, who has compiled this book was sometimes with us, and although a very young lad I like to feel that this developed his appreciation of Gwentian scene, and also started his interest in photographic recording.

Fred Hando has often been accused of presenting legends to his readers as historical facts. With this I do not agree for the old stories, however fianciful, are the spice of history. Fred, I am sure, was only recording them, and who is to say that the stories handed down from generation to generation are less reliable than the deductions of the historian trying to make his dates and data tally.

Fred approached everything with a youthful zest that belied his years. I still have many vivid memories of the many journies we made together; of the momentous day we found, hidden behind a shop fitting in Cross Street, Abergavenny, a mediaeval mural of the 'Adoration of the Magi.' It was probably once in a room above the shop where fugitive Papist priests performed the forbidden rites of Catholic Mass. It is now in the Town Museum. Then the day we found another secret room, used for the same purpose, at ancient Trefor, a house in north-east Gwent.

Places wild and atmospheric gave pleasure to Fred, such as the wind-swept lonely upland moors of Fforest Fawr, a bleak wind-swept area criss-crossed with ancient tracks and Roman marching roads signposted, in many instances, by prehistoric stones. The precarious drive along a narrow track, some three hundred feet above the Clydach gorge he also found exciting.

I particularly remember one of the last journies we made together, one along the old drovers' road across the Cambrian Mountains. Fred, crooning with delight, and regaling me with a picture of the wild scene as I needed all my concentration in keeping our car on the very steep and winding mountain track.

Fred Hando, *'that Man of Gwent'*, author, artist, musician and raconteur, but above all a friend and a *'good companion.'* My memories of the joy in his companionship will never be forgotten.

Bill Barber.
July 1987

Arthur Machen — a pencil drawing by Fred Hando.

"Our author has roamed by hidden woods and tracked unsuspected streams, and trodden many unchronicled paths and byways, pacing the turf of sudden hills that are known to most only from afar, and becoming familiar with unconjectured valleys, deep and concealed from common sight. And those old houses, of fifteenth, sixteenth and seventeenth century, aslar, manorial, armigerous in their day, now housing farmers for the most part — places such as Kemeys on the old road from Caerleon — these, whether in the grave shadow of the valley, or shining on the hillside, this pilgrim of Gwent has viewed and recorded by word and by line. He has gone abroad in search of wonder and enchantment, and finding these abounding has set them fairly on his page."

Arthur Machen.

INDEX

"The townsman, however well-informed, should never boast about his countryside knowledge. He may possibly possess encycolpaedic information about his town, but to know fully any part of the country demands residence in that part."

Llangwm Uchaf

"When we stand on the green hillsides of Gwent and look down on a valley church, our hearts grow within us. The trees bend in benediction, the rounded meadows are threaded with church-paths, the bells from the grey tower fill the valley air, and God is no longer remote."

Kemeys Inferior (before demolition)

ACKNOWLEDGEMENTS

I am grateful to the Editor of the South Wales Argus for permission to use extracts from the many articles and illustrations which appeared in that journal and submitted by Fred Hando on a regular basis.

Also I am grateful to Mrs Susan Hando for allowing me to purchase the copyright of Fred Hando's work and also to several other members of the Hando family who have given assistance in various ways.

I thank my father, Bill Barber, Mr. John Collet and Mr R.F. Stevens for their memories of Fred Hando.

To Mr. and Mrs. Bramley of Caerleon I give my appreciation for allowing me to borrow their collection of Fred Hando articles which provided me with the bulk of my source material.

Chris Barber 1987

Artist at work!

BOOKS BY FRED HANDO

Rambles in Gwent.
The Pleasant Land of Gwent.
Journeys in Gwent.
Monmouthshire Sketchbook.
Here and there in Monmouthshire.
Monmouth Town Sketch Book.
Out and About in Monmouthshire.

OTHER TITLES BY CHRIS BARBER

Walks in the Brecon Beacons.
Exploring the Waterfall Country.
Ghosts of Wales.
Exploring the Brecon Beacons National Park.
Exploring Gwent.
Mysterious Wales.
More Mysterious Wales.
Cordell Country.
The Romance of the Welsh Mountains.

Sugar Loaf and Skirrid Fawr from the Bettws Newydd road.

And what of the people who live in Gwent? We have in our towns as in our countryside many of the ancient stock. You will find our people self-contained, proud of their town or village, proud of their church, retaining much of the old-time family life, and possessed of a salty humour. They will give you a certain calm welcome to their home or their inn; they will listen as well as talk; and as time passes, you, the newcomer, will discover that in their company you have changed; they remain as they were, for the true man of Gwent knows that priceless gift of God — inner repose.